This Light of Ours

This Light of Ours

Activist Photographers of the Civil Rights Movement

Edited by Leslie G. Kelen

Essays by Julian Bond, Clayborne Carson, and Matt Herron

Text by Charles E. Cobb, Jr.

University Press of Mississippi   Jackson

www.upress.state.ms.us

The University Press of Mississippi is a member of the Association of American University Presses.

Photograph on pages 1 and 2: Matt Herron, Alabama, 1965

Library of Congress Cataloging-in-Publication Data

This light of ours : activist photographers of the civil rights movement / edited by Leslie G. Kelen ; essays by Julian Bond, Clayborne Carson, and Matt Herron ; text by Charles E. Cobb, Jr.
    p. cm.
  Includes bibliographical references and index.
  ISBN 978-1-61703-171-7 (cloth : alk. paper) — ISBN 978-1-61703-172-4 (ebook) 1. African Americans—Civil rights—History—20th century—Pictorial works. 2. Civil rights movements—United States—History—20th century—Pictorial works. 3. United States—Race relations—History—20th century—Pictorial works. 4. Southern States—Race relations—History—20th century—Pictorial works. 5. Photographers—Political activity—United States—History—20th century. 6. Political activists—United States—History—20th century. 7. Student Nonviolent Coordinating Committee (U.S.)—History. 8. Photographers—United States—Interviews. 9. Political activists—United States—Interviews. I. Kelen, Leslie G., 1949– II. Bond, Julian, 1940– III. Carson, Clayborne, 1944– IV. Herron, Matt, 1931– V. Cobb, Charles E., Jr.
  E185.615.T495 2011
  305.800973—dc23   2011016247

British Library Cataloging-in-Publication Data available

DEDICATION

Publication of this book was supported generously by the
Board of Directors of the George S. and Dolores Doré Eccles Foundation,
in honor and memory of fellow board member
Alonzo W. "Lon" Watson, Jr.
(1922–2005)
whose service for more than 25 years was highlighted
by his dedication to building a more just and compassionate society.

Board of Directors
Spencer F. Eccles, Chairman & CEO
Lisa Eccles, President
Robert M. Graham, Secretary, Treasurer & General Counsel

Contents

9   Preface and Acknowledgments   *Leslie G. Kelen*

13   Foreword   *Julian Bond*

19   Photographing Civil Rights   *Matt Herron*

The Photographs
Text by *Charles E. Cobb, Jr.*

28   Part One: Black Life

60   Part Two: Organizing for Freedom

127   Part Three: State and Local Terror

162   Part Four: Meredith March against Fear and Black Power

191   Reflection: How I First Saw King and Found the Movement   *Clayborne Carson*

The Photographers: Interviews and Biographies

206   Tamio Wakayama

212   Herbert Randall

217   Maria Varela

223   George Ballis

228   Bob Fitch

233   Matt Herron

239   Bob Fletcher

241   David Prince

243   Bob Adelman

245   Recommended Reading

247   Index

This little light of mine

I'm going to let it shine

Oh, this little light of mine

I'm going to let it shine . . .

Let it shine, let it shine, let it shine. . . .

—Movement anthem and African American gospel song,
written by Harry Dixon Loes

Preface and Acknowledgments

Leslie G. Kelen

Anyone who has worked long on a book project knows that a preface is written after a project is completed as a way of providing a synopsis of the effort and an introduction to the reader. The preface to *This Light of Ours: Activist Photographers of the Civil Rights Movement* isn't an exception. Nevertheless, in preparing to write it, I found myself reluctant to admit the project is over. In large part, this is because the project has been enormously transformative. It has provided all of us at the Center for Documentary Expression & Art (CDEA) who worked on it with a new appreciation for the complexity of the Civil Rights Movement and a deeper understanding and regard for the thousands of people (young and older, known and relatively unknown) who carried out its actions.

Personally, I feel fortunate to have been able to form a relationship with the photographers whose work is in this book and to have the honor to participate, in some small way, in telling their stories. The Civil Rights or Southern Freedom Movement is unquestionably one of the shining moments in the history of this nation. It was—and remains—one of the moments when people (as photographer Matt Herron and others observed) moved "beyond" their usual capacities and risked their safeties and, in some cases, their lives to realize the civil and human rights of African Americans and, by implication and example, other disenfranchised American people. And as the photographs and accompanying text in this book demonstrate, the movement's achievements continue to reverberate throughout our communities as good tidings and as powerful reminders of our capacity to stand up against the evils of racism. So, reader, please consider this preface as both a reluctant admission of work completed and as invitation to you to experience it and to use its lessons to enrich your life and the lives of others. As SNCC communications director Julian Bond writes in the foreword that follows: "The photographs you see here . . . remind us of what we were—and what we hope we can be again."

This Light of Ours: Activist Photographers of the Civil Rights Movement presents the work of nine men and women who lived and worked in the American Civil Rights Movement between 1963 and 1968. (The book is also the catalogue to a major traveling exhibition of the same title.) As a group, the photographers represent two generations of Americans from an array of ethnic identities (i.e., African American, Greek, Irish, Japanese, Jewish, Mexican, and WASP) as well as people from both coasts and the veritable heartland. Unlike the photojournalists who entered the movement on assignment for magazines and newspapers and left after completing their work, each of these photographers chose to live in and participate in the movement as an activist. Herb Randall, David Prince, and George Ballis stayed directly engaged in the movement for several months. Bob Adelman, Bob Fitch, Bob Fletcher, Matt Herron, Maria Varela, and Tamio Wakayama stayed in the movement anywhere from a year to five years. Three of the nine—Fletcher, Varela, and Wakayama—became photographers as a result of the movement. The other six came to the movement with varying degrees of training and experience. The majority of these photographers did not then and do not now see themselves primarily as photographers but as "activists" or "organizers" with cameras. And this self-definition is important to keep in mind when considering this book and what it represents; each of these people participated in the Southern Freedom Movement because it was what their lives, their deepest instincts, called for. And as the interviews and biographies suggest, their activism—with and without cameras—continued long after their participation in the movement ended.

Seven of the nine photographers were either staff members or close associates of the Student Nonviolent Coordinating Committee (SNCC—pronounced "snick"). The other two worked for or were engaged with the Southern Christian Leadership Conference (SCLC) and the Congress of Racial Equality (CORE). Of the major civil rights organizations, SNCC was, it turns out, uniquely farsighted in its usage of photographers and photographs. Soon after its 1960 founding in Raleigh, North Carolina, this student-led organization invited photographers to be an integral part of their communications effort. And by the summer of 1964, when the bulk of the photographers in this book arrived on the scene, SNCC had a working darkroom in Atlanta and was fielding a team of photographers to document the organization's activities and to use photos to convey the aims and struggles of the movement to the nation.

Of the 151 black-and-white photographs presented in this book the majority convey SNCC's "bottom-up" organizing techniques, voter registration efforts, and community empowerment campaigns. In fact, it is not a stretch to say that this book offers a unique visual narrative of SNCC's activities and development in the Deep South states of Mississippi and Alabama between the years 1963 and 1966. The very construct of the book reflects these activities both chronologically and thematically. The documentation of SCLC and CORE carried out, respectively, by Bob Fitch and Bob Adelman do not, on the whole, shift focus away from SNCC so much as complement, deepen, and expand

it. And as the photographs indicate, the Deep South was the battleground on which Americans in the 1960s struggled to establish the nation's new moral direction. In *This Light of Ours*, we see this battleground primarily from the perspective of SNCC's young activists working together with local people and their partners in SCLC and CORE.

This Light of Ours is organized into four interrelated sections—"Black Life," "Organizing for Freedom," "State and Local Terror," and "Meredith March against Fear and Black Power"—and presents, in the words of photographer Maria Varela, what activist photographers saw, did, experienced in terms of push back from white supremacists, and implicitly and explicitly accomplished. A reader coming to these photographs for the first time can expect to travel, consequently, alongside several photographers in each section and to experience or perceive the movement through their eyes. For example, in "Black Life," the book's first section, the reader will travel with Adelman, Fitch, Fletcher, Herron, Varela, and Wakayama and will move primarily through Mississippi and Alabama (with additional photos from Georgia, Louisiana, and Texas), encountering black people at home, at work, at church, at play, and in some movement activities. Images convey, in large part, people's resilience, humor, strength, determination, verve, beauty, and distress. The photographers did not see black people primarily as victims, although their suffering is evident in the photos, but as actors in their own liberation.

In "Organizing for Freedom," the book's second and longest section, the reader will engage SNCC's community organizing, voter registration, and party building efforts from the 1963 Mississippi mock vote, through the unprecedented 1964 Summer Project (also called "Freedom Summer") and its national aftermath, all the way to the fall of 1966, when black people in Alabama (supported by the newly passed 1965 Voting Rights Act) voted for the first time for candidates put forth by their own Lowndes County Freedom Organization, also known as the Lowndes County Black Panther

Party. The "Organizing for Freedom" section makes evident the nexus between local and national politics and between national policies and local conditions.

In "State and Local Terror," the book's third section, the reader will confront the varied expressions of white supremacy in Alabama and Mississippi as well as Georgia and Louisiana. These disturbing images (which include a section of photos from the 1968 funeral of Dr. Martin Luther King, Jr.) present the "state" acting at various levels of government to intimidate and destroy the movement, local whites bluntly expressing their racist outlooks, and black people responding to the onslaught. Finally, in "Meredith March against Fear and Black Power," the book's fourth section, the reader will see both the movement's last great march and one of its complex and controversial outcomes. "Black Power," or the empowerment of black people, was SNCC's primary purpose, yet Stokely Carmichael's impassioned presentation of the concept on the march frightened whites and caused deep divisions within the movement. Ironically, the vision unfolding in the Black Power concept telescoped the postmovement phase of national life when *new* power for black people *was* realized through movement-caused changes in American institutions and attitudes.

A word of explanation is in order here about the text that accompanies the photographs. Charlie Cobb, Jr., a SNCC veteran and the project's historical consultant, wrote the book's section headings and photo captions (with input from exhibition curator Matt Herron). A former SNCC field secretary and a student of the movement, Cobb gives readers a passionate and penetrating insider's view of SNCC methods, strategies, and achievements. Julian Bond, SNCC's communications director and later chairman of the national NAACP, wrote the foreword wherein he describes SNCC's unique role in and impact on the movement and its effective usage of photographs. Matt Herron's essay vividly evokes how activist photographers came to work in the movement, how they

dealt with the unique dangers of working in the South, and what they sought to accomplish. And movement historian Dr. Clayborne Carson provides an extended meditation on encountering SNCC as a young man and its impact on his personal and professional life. Carson's essay also recounts SNCC's organizational development, major accomplishments, and lasting legacies. Cumulatively, the book's text offers a historical framework that deepens our engagement with and understanding of the photographs, the photographers, and the movement.

There are biographies of all nine photographers as well as extended interviews with six of the nine in the book's closing section. I conducted the interviews of the photographers in their homes and edited them for this publication. In each interview, a photographer recalls how he/she found the movement, what they did within it, and how the movement affected them. The interviews offer intimate and nuanced accounts of participation in both SNCC and SCLC, as well as revealing glimpses of individuals on the front lines of social change in America. Transcripts of the full interviews will be available on the Center for Documentary Expression & Art Web site. George "Elfie" Ballis, the oldest of the nine, passed away on September 24, 2010, at his home; he was eighty-five years old at the time of his death. He won't be here to see his work live alongside the work of his comrades. But of all the photographers in this book, Elfie (as he preferred to be called) knew and celebrated the project's goals of presenting the movement anew and empowering the next generation of American activists.

This Light of Ours: Activist Photographers of the Civil Rights Movement is, I believe, the first major collection of images to present SNCC's organizing methods and movement achievements and to convey, in the process, a more grassroots-based portrait of the Civil Rights Movement than we are used to encountering through the mainstream media. It is a vision of the movement that does not single out charismatic heroes and leaders, but helps us understand that freedom's light shines brighter in the United States today because of the combined contributions of thousands of "ordinary" Americans—young black organizers, northern student volunteers, grassroots leaders, local people in local networks, activist photographers, and many others—who took it upon themselves to change the nation.

· · ·

I would like to acknowledge the people whose contributions were vital to assuring the intellectual, historical, and aesthetic viability of this project. First, I want to thank author, curator, and gallery owner Steven Kasher for suggesting the initial idea for this project, connecting CDEA with exhibit curator Matt Herron, and providing guidance on the selection of photographs. Second, I want to recognize CDEA's staff and local consultants—Kent Miles, Doris Mason, Mary Lee Peters, Norm Judd, Gilberto Schaefer, Francie Wyss, Chris Frazier, and Bryce Olsen—and CDEA's board of trustees—Dr. Hank Liese, Archie Archuleta, Jean Brady, Larry Cesspooch, Kathy Christy, Jeff Davis, Bob Miller, Fahina Pasi, Dr. Natasha Rapoport, Allen Roberts, and Dr. Ron Smelser; you were each there from the beginning when this project was a concept and you contributed your skills when most needed to make sure it would succeed. Third, I would like to thank CDEA's national consultants, advisors, and collaborators—Matt Herron, Charlie Cobb, Jr., Judy Richardson, Maria Varela, Julian Bond, Dr. Clayborne Carson, Dr. Emilye Crosby, Dr. John Dittmer, Dr. Hasan Jeffries, Dr. Wesley Hogan and photographers Bob Adelman, George Ballis, Bob Fitch, Bob Fletcher, David Prince, Herbert Randall, and Tamio Wakayama; you collectively helped develop the project's content and shape what I hope will be its enduring vision. Fourth, I want to thank the staff and board of The Leonardo, Salt Lake City's new art, science, and technology center at which the exhibition of *This Light of Ours: Activist Photographers of the Civil Rights Movement* will debut; your belief in the project and willingness to

establish a human rights gallery in the new facility is an expression of true collaboration.

I also want to acknowledge the people and organizations whose support were vital to assuring the financial viability of the project. First, I thank Bruce W. Bastian and Michael Marriott of the B. W. Bastian Foundation, whose generous financial support and commitment to tell the stories of human rights activists from the 1960s black Civil Rights Movement to the present-day Gay and Lesbian Movement are an inspiration and a model of moral action. Second, I want to thank former Salt Lake City mayor Ross "Rocky" Anderson, who was not afraid to bring human rights activism into his office and politics and who facilitated CDEA's meeting with Bruce Bastian. Third, I thank Utah legislators Jackie Biskupski and David Litvack, Pastor France Davis, attorney and educator Jim Richards, wise counselor Alexander Morrison, and current Salt Lake City mayor Ralph Becker for selflessly stepping in at critical junctures in the process to help CDEA gather financial support. Fourth, I want to acknowledge the many national and local organizations who provided invaluable financial support, such as the National Endowment for the Arts; Salt Lake County Government; Salt Lake County Zoo, Arts, and Parks Program; Williams Corporation; Zions Bank; the George S. and Dolores Doré Eccles Foundation; the Tanner Trust and Tanner Co.; Qwest; Goldman Sachs; and Snell & Wilmer.

Finally, I would like to thank Craig Gill, assistant director and editor-in-chief of the University Press of Mississippi, for his unwavering support of this project; my wife and life partner, Dr. Joyce Green Kelen, for believing in my efforts (and letting me be the "happy genius of my household"); my sons, David and Jonathan, for having the courage to live their own lives; and my mother, Ilona Kelen, and my sister, Eva Kelen Weiss, for keeping alive the connection between the worlds that were and the worlds that are and may yet come to be.

Foreword

Julian Bond

A historian wrote of the Student Nonviolent Coordinating Committee (SNCC): "Central aspects of the social movement embodied by SNCC were its nurture of a media consciousness among its activists and an insistence on the historicity of the struggle itself—a preoccupation of leaving a record as being part of the organization's collective awareness.[1]"

Fifty years after SNCC's founding, the publication and photo exhibit *This Light of Ours: Activist Photographers of the Civil Rights Movement* confirms the importance of SNCC's awareness of image—its own and that of the struggle itself.

In providing a visual record of the organization and the ethos in which it operated, these photographs help us understand SNCC as no text alone can.

John F. Kennedy said that compared to Martin Luther King's Southern Christian Leadership Conference (SCLC), SNCC workers were "real sons of bitches."

SNCC began in April 1960 at a conference of students, mostly black, called by Ella Baker. Baker, a longtime civil rights activist, became an important advisor to the nascent SNCC, effectively guiding it away from the personality cult that typified King-worship at the SCLC, where she then worked, and the bureaucracy of the NAACP, where she had worked in the past, toward group democracy, with every member having his or her say.

SNCC's "members"[2] adopted collective decision-making, which took account of every point of view, and organized communities to act in their own behalf rather than depend almost exclusively on the protest strategy of SCLC. This resulted in an organization whose accomplishments and achievements in its short life far surpassed those of older, more conservative organizations.

Within a year of its founding, SNCC evolved from a committee coordinating student protests to a hands-on organization helping local leadership in rural and small-town communities across the South participate in a variety of protests and political and economic organizing campaigns, setting SNCC apart from the civil rights mainstream of the 1960s.

Its members, youth, and independence enabled SNCC to remain close to grassroots currents that rapidly escalated the southern movement from sit-ins to Freedom Rides to voter drives to political organizing.

By 1965, SNCC fielded the largest staff of any civil rights organization operating in the South. It had organized antisegregation protests and voter registration projects in every southern state. It had built two independent political parties and organized labor unions and agricultural cooperatives. It gave the existing movement for women's liberation new energy. It inspired and trained the activists who began the "New Left." It helped expand the limits of political debate within black America and broadened the focus of the Civil Rights Movement.

Unlike mainstream civil rights groups, which sought integration of blacks into the existing order, SNCC sought structural changes in American society itself.[3]

For much of its early history, SNCC battled against the fear which had kept southern rural blacks from aggressively organizing and acting in their own behalf. It strengthened or built aggressive, locally led movements in the communities where it worked.

SNCC workers offered themselves as a protective barrier between private and state-sponsored terror and the local communities where SNCC staffers lived and worked.

SNCC staffers frequently were the first *paid* civil rights workers to headquarter themselves in isolated rural communities, daring to "take the message of freedom into areas where the bigger civil rights organizations fear to tread."[4]

"Freedom Summer 1964" brought one thousand mostly white volunteers to Mississippi. They registered voters, built community centers, and staffed twenty-eight "Freedom Schools."

Over the next several years, SNCC backed first-time black candidates for Congress who ran in Georgia, Alabama, Virginia, and North Carolina.[5]

My campaign for the Georgia House of Representatives in 1965 was an attempt to take the techniques SNCC had learned in the rural South into an urban setting, and to carry forward SNCC's belief that grassroots politics could provide answers to problems faced by America's urban blacks.

In keeping with SNCC's style, a platform was developed in consultation with the voters.

When the legislature twice rejected me, objecting to my support of SNCC's antiwar position, the resulting campaigns gave SNCC chances to successfully test its critique of American imperialism at the ballot box.

The campaign enabled SNCC to provide a political voice for the politically inarticulate and impotent black poor.

In 1966 in Alabama, SNCC helped to create a black political party called the Lowndes County Freedom Organization (LCFO), "an independent political party which would prove to be a factor in Alabama politics for years to come. . . . The political consciousness of some of Alabama's blacks had been raised to another level."[6]

Just as its concern for social change had never been limited to the southern states alone, SNCC's concern for human rights had long extended beyond the borders of the United States.

It had linked the fight of American blacks with the struggle for African independence from its first public statements.

There are many reasons for the demise of this important organization. The current of nationalism, ever present in black America, widened at the end of the 1960s to become a rushing torrent which swept away the hopeful notion of "black and white together" that the decade's beginning had promised.

SNCC's white staff members were asked to leave the organization and devote their energies to organizing in white communities; some agreed, but most believed this action repudiated the movement's hopeful call to "Americans all, side by equal side."

For many on the staff, both white and black, nearly a decade's worth of hard work at irregular, subsistence-level pay, under an atmosphere of constant tension, interrupted by jailings, beatings, and official and private terror, proved too much.

Throughout its brief history, SNCC insisted on group-centered leadership and community-based politics. It made clear the connection between economic power and racial oppression. It refused to define racism as solely southern, to describe racial inequality as caused by irrational prejudice alone, or to limit its struggle solely to guaranteeing legal equality. It challenged American imperialism while mainstream civil rights organizations were silent or curried favor with President Lyndon Johnson, condemning SNCC's linkage of domestic poverty and racism with overseas adventurism.

SNCC refused to apply political tests to its membership or supporters, opposing the Red-baiting which other organizations and leaders endorsed or condoned. It created an atmosphere of expectation and anticipation among the people with whom it worked, trusting them to make decisions about their own lives.

For SNCC, politics encompassed not only electoral races, but also organizing political parties, labor unions, producer cooperatives, and alternative schools.

It initially sought to liberalize southern politics by organizing and enfranchising blacks. But it also sought to liberalize the ends of political participation by enlarging the issues of political debate to include the economic and foreign policy concerns of American blacks.

SNCC's articulation and advocacy of Black Power redefined the relationship between black Americans and white power. No longer would political equity be considered a privilege; it had become a right.

Another SNCC legacy is the destruction of the psychological shackles which had kept black southerners in physical and mental peonage; the Student Nonviolent Coordinating Committee helped to break those chains forever.

What began fifty years ago is not just history. It was a part of a mighty movement that started many years ago and that continues to this day.

The photographs you see here preserve that history and remind us of work accomplished and work yet to be done.

James Forman, SNCC's executive director, constantly urged us to "write it down." I never heard him say, "Take a picture of it," but recording our daily goings-on was implicit in his leadership. A devotee of W. E. B. Du Bois and a former high school teacher and newspaper reporter for the *Chicago Defender*, he understood how important it was to record and document SNCC's activities.

Thus the SNCC archives are filled with reports recounting the daily activities of our field secretaries, offering scholars and others a rich record of day-to-day doings not normally available to the public.

Uniquely among its civil rights organizational contemporaries, SNCC employed photographers, stocked darkrooms in Atlanta, Georgia, and Tougaloo, Mississippi, sent photographers to train with famed photographer Richard Avedon, employed photography in exceptional ways, and produced photographers who are distinguished in the field today.

SNCC "used" photography in ordinary and extraordinary ways. "SNCC photos have been used in court cases, in books, magazines, and newspapers, on TV and have been organized into traveling exhibitions. The photographers are mostly self-trained and work under combat-like conditions. Not only are they constantly harassed, but their equipment is often destroyed or confiscated by racist police officials and individuals."[7]

SNCC photographer Bobby Fletcher described how they were used. Requests for pictures came from within and without the United States: ". . . from within the country from fundraising groups and support groups, and from left-wing liberal and left-wing publications, yes. But from outside, and also from time to time from AP and UPI. Also we were getting requests from more established newspapers and magazines in England and France and Italy, and so we had all these requests that would come in and it was our job to pull from the stuff that we had put together and send them out."[8]

As head of SNCC's communications department, I know firsthand that we utilized our photographers' outputs in many ways.

SNCC's idea of photography was functional; it was to provide pictures for SNCC's propaganda. Our photographers took this function and made it art. Their pictures became illustrations in numerous brochures, pamphlets, educational and fund-raising filmstrips, and in our weekly newsletter, the *Student Voice*. Thousands of copies of the *Voice* were distributed to our southern projects in various states and to our supporters in the North. The photos added immediacy and made more compelling reports of SNCC activity and accounts of the routine brutality and cruelty our workers and the people with whom we worked experienced.

We created and sold wonderful posters with our photos—the first civil rights organization to do so.

We included the photos in the press releases we regularly mailed out, giving away prints by now-famous photographers that today sell for thousands of dollars.

SNCC's first photo exhibit, called "NOW," opened at New York's Visual Arts Gallery in July 1965. Richard Avedon was one of the honorary chairmen.

A second show, called "US," was a seventy-four-photo touring show the organization created.[9]

George Love, then director of the Heliograph Gallery in New York, and Betty Brown, editor of *Popular Photography* magazine, designed the show. It opened in February 1967 at New York's Countee Cullen Library, sponsored by the Schomburg Collection, with photojournalist Gordon Parks as sponsor. Both shows toured widely.

The list of photographers employed by or associated with SNCC is lengthy.[10]

In an undated memorandum from the SNCC archives, Julius Lester wrote of ambitious plans for the SNCC photo department, "work in progress on four projects":

The Day They Came To Vote, "a booklet of 10 to 15 pages comprising 26 photographs of the May 3 primary in Lowndes County";

A Lowndes County calendar—"It will consist of photographs of Lowndes County, including the candidates of the LCFO";

A SNCC calendar—"it will consist of twelve photographs of the South, include dates from Negro history and 'the movement' and short quotations from the works of black writers"; and

An engagement calendar modeled on the Museum of Modern Art and U.N. calendars. "It would consist of 104 photographs, two weeks to a page and quotations from the writings of black writers. It would be aimed at the Negro middle class and college campuses."

Unfortunately, only the final two of these projects were completed and in more modest formats than originally envisioned. The other projects never came to fruition.

That's one reason why these photos are so precious—they are present, here and now, for you to see and appreciate.

I remember seeing some of these and other movement photos for the first time and marveling at how powerful they were. They are more powerful now. They summon the bravery of ordinary people called to do extraordinary things, to risk life and limb to secure democracy for themselves and their neighbors.

They remind us of what we were—and what we hope we can be again.

Notes

1. Iris Schmeisser, "Camera at the Grassroots: The Student Nonviolent Coordinating Committee and the Politics of Visual Representation," in *The Civil Rights Movement Revisited: Critical Perspectives on the Struggle for Racial Equality in the United States*, ed. Patrick B. Miller, Therese Frey Steffen, and Elizabeth Schafer-Wunsche (Hamburg: Lit: 2001).

2. SNCC had no formal "members" like the NAACP or the Congress of Racial Equality (CORE) and no dues or membership cards or requirements; rather its "members" were the people who showed up every day to do whatever work they had volunteered for or were assigned. Some were paid starvation-level wages based on need. As a married man with a growing family, I was the highest paid employee during my tenure, but my salary never exceeded sixty dollars a week.

3. Papers of the Student Nonviolent Coordinating Committee; Clayborne Carson, *In Struggle: SNCC and the Black Awakening of the 1960s* (Harvard University Press, 1981); Howard Zinn, *SNCC: The New Abolitionists* (Beacon Press, 1965); James Forman, *The Making of Black Revolutionaries* (Open Hand Press, 1985); James Forman, *1967: High Tide of Black Resistance* (SNCC, 1967); Cleveland Sellers and Robert Terrell, *The River of No Return* (William Morrow & Co., 1973); Emily Stoper, *The Student Nonviolent Coordinating Committee* (Carlson Publishing Co., 1989); "Dear Friend," fund-raising letter from SNCC Chairman John Lewis (1965).

4. *Atlanta Inquirer*, March 1962.

5. Stoper, pp. 14–15.

6. Hardy Thomas Frye, "The Rise of a Black Political Party: Institutional Consequences of Emerging Political Consciousness" (Ph.D. thesis, University of California, Berkeley, 1975), p. 68.

7. Harvey S. Zucker, solicitation letter for SNCC photo. "More than Richard Avedon, there was a guy named Harvey Zucker . . . a photographer. He had a studio in New York in NOHO. . . . He would

show us about developing, and he's the one I remember more. With Matt [Herron] I learned about the zone scale. With Harvey I learned about burning and dodging and diagramming out a photograph and planning out what it was gonna look like at the end of the day. . . ." Leslie Kelen, interview with Bobby Fletcher, October 8, 2009.

8. Bobby Fletcher interview.

9. Photographers for "US" were Charles Cobb, Fred Devan, Robert Fletcher, George Frye, Doug Harris, Rufus Hinton, Julius Lester, Danny Lyon, Herb Randall, Buford Smith, William Squire, Mary Varela, Clifford Vaughs, Tom Wakayama, and Shawn Walker.

10. Another list of photographers—not all employed by SNCC but found in the SNCC archives under the heading "Film Job Numbers and Disposition"—includes Robert Weaver, Norris McNamara, Mike Sayer, Joyce Barrett, Phil Davis, D. Crowder, Matt Herron, Bill Light, Dave Prince, Mack Suckle, Tracy Sugarman, Francis Mitchell, Pete Marx, Georgia Ballis, Herbert Randall, Lee Garrett, J. V. Henry, Jerry DeMuth, Dorothy Teal, Robert Mants, Philip Moore, Julian Bond, Rufus Hinton, and H. Kaminsky. The list includes a description of where each of an astounding 1,065 rolls of film taken by these photographers was shot. Not included, to our eternal sadness, is the film itself. SNCC Archives, Martin Luther King, Jr., Library, Atlanta, Georgia.

Photographing Civil Rights

Matt Herron

The mantle of civil rights photography was not a one-size-fits-all garment. There were as many styles to this work as there were civil rights photographers, or at least so it appears looking back over the years and reconstructing the experiences of these activist photographers of the sixties. But if most of us approached our task clad in our own personal outlook and strategies, the opportunities and problems we faced were remarkably similar.

To begin with, we moved through an extraordinarily rich visual environment. As anyone who has looked at civil rights photography will instantly recognize, the faces, the landscapes, the confrontations all yielded immensely powerful images. For many of us those intense, brief years gave rise to our best photographic work, and for all of us those times remain among the most profound, formative experiences of our lives.

Tamio Wakayama remembers the joy he felt driving through that tunnel of a road north of Jackson, all overgrown with kudzu vine, and seeing it broaden out above Yazoo City into the vast expanse of the Mississippi Delta. "It was like reentering the land of my boyhood in southwest Ontario in Canada," he remembered. "Those broad fields studded with sharecropper shacks seemed to have that same organic integrity— the shacks not so much man-made as just growing out of the soil. It felt like my home." And that's the way he photographed it—lonely structures married to the earth, black farmers raising food for their families. But of course that was only one way of looking at the Delta. Maria Varela found a darker vision: barren mud-choked roads, crumbling plantation shacks, lively but impoverished kids dancing for her camera. And for all

of us, the core of our work as well as the root source of the movement's strength lay in those cohesive black communities, centered around church and bound together by common struggle. There we found the faces upon which were written histories of hard living, but also of resilience, humor, and, above all, hope. Truly, it was a visual feast for anyone with eyes to see. But why did it sometimes *not* seem like a feast to us? Perhaps because our work could be hard and sometimes very dangerous.

Unlike the photojournalists, who viewed a quite different civil rights movement through the lens of guaranteed assignments and comfortable expense accounts, we operated with meager resources, sleeping on floors, living out of suitcases and the trunks of our cars. We bought our 35mm Tri X in hundred-foot rolls, spooling it out at night into film cassettes, which allowed us to shoot our pictures for a penny a frame. Our darkrooms were a precious resource—we lacked the luxury of shipping our film to professional labs in New York—and often they were temporary affairs, set up in a bathroom that continued to serve a dual purpose. And automobiles were a constant problem. They broke down and had to be repaired, not only to get us from A to B, but sometimes to save our hide in a high-speed chase.

Bob Fitch recalls his financial arrangement with Martin Luther King's Southern Christian Leadership Conference. He took over as a volunteer photographer for SCLC when they found it too dangerous to send black photographers into the field to shoot the project pictures they were supplying to African American newspapers in the North. "I became a sort of one-man

Associated Press. I covered everything—from camera click to stamp lick, as I called it. I shot the pictures, souped the film, made the prints, wrote the captions and mailed them out. SCLC covered my travel expenses and they paid me fifteen dollars a week room and board. That was it. But I could walk down to the newsstand on Tuesday afternoon and see my pictures in every black newspaper."

Some of us were staff members of the Student Nonviolent Coordinating Committee and lived on SNCC's standard weekly stipend of $9.64 (after deductions!). Others, like myself, supported families on occasional news assignments from northern magazines, which allowed us to photograph for the movement. Considering SNCC's scanty funds, it is remarkable that Executive Director Jim Forman was willing to devote resources to building a team of photographers, a professional darkroom, and a communications unit headed by Julian Bond (working with Mary King) that issued press releases and sent photographs and research reports to media and liberal outlets in the North. Forman uniquely understood the importance of building northern support through regular reports on southern suppression and movement efforts to end it. And photographs were by far the most dramatic way to convey that message.

We came from all walks of photographic life, and from other walks as well. I moved to Mississippi with my family in the summer of 1963—the only family with children to move south and join the movement. As a committed pacifist, I had been organizing peace demonstrations for a Quaker group in Philadelphia, but the sit-ins were a siren song calling us south. Both my wife, Jeannine, and I believed in nonviolence as a way of life, and we felt we could be more effective working in Mississippi where nonviolence was undergoing its severest test. I was already launched on the beginnings of a photographic career. With a picture in *Life* and a major story in *Look*, I had begun to establish relationships with many magazine editors in New York, and I hoped to supply them with pithy picture story ideas from the heart of Mississippi. But I soon

learned they had scant interest in my ideas; they were happy, however, to call me when there was trouble.

George Ballis joined me in June of 1964 as part of a team of documentary photographers that I had put together to document the process of social change during that pivotal summer. He came from Fresno in California's Central Valley where he edited a small newspaper covering migrant labor issues, and where he shot all the pictures for his one-man operation. He returned to California that fall to become one of the principal photographers documenting Cesar Chavez's United Farm Workers movement.

Bob Fitch also came from California, a divinity graduate of the Pacific School of Religion who had become disillusioned with organized religion's lack of involvement with the social issues of the day. He shot pictures for the Glide Foundation in San Francisco and raised funds to send civil rights workers south. Finally he decided to go himself. "I was theologically trained and I had a strong belief that humans can command God's presence by going through certain rituals. And this was one of them: the God of Justice at work."

Herb Randall discovered photography in 1955 when friends took him to see Edward Steichen's groundbreaking exhibition, *The Family of Man*, at the Museum of Modern Art in New York. Later he studied with Harold Feinstein, and in 1964 won a John Hay Whitney fellowship to photograph life in the South. He joined the Mississippi Summer Project and spent July and August in Hattiesburg documenting voter registration efforts, Freedom Schools, and some of the violence that erupted in this Klan-dominated section of the state. Randall remembers joking with Rabbi Arthur Lelyveld, who was questioning whether short-term volunteers like himself made any difference, that all the rabbi had to do was walk downtown and get his butt kicked. The next morning his joke turned to horror when the rabbi was attacked with a tire iron, and Randall found himself trying to staunch the stricken man's heavy bleeding. Looking up at him, the rabbi said, "Take my picture."

Maria Varela's Mexican roots extended back to the

Mexican Revolution when her grandfather, fleeing violence, moved his family across the border to San Antonio, and later onward to New Jersey in a further flight from Texas racism. In college she began organizing students, going around to campuses, giving talks, trying to get young people involved with the Civil Rights Movement. Meanwhile, she was carrying, unanswered, a letter from a friend in Atlanta urging her to come south personally to work with SNCC. Finally she responded, and soon found herself living underground in Selma, Alabama, conducting literacy classes for would-be black voters in one of the most repressive towns in the South.

Maria became a photographer out of frustration. Unable to find literacy materials that mirrored the life experiences of southern blacks, she took up a camera and began creating them herself. Like George Ballis, she began to think of herself not as a photographer, but as an organizer with a camera, working in that mode because people responded most directly to pictures. She came to me for rudimentary instruction, and in the process discovered photography's wider lineage.

Around Matt's studio were photography books about Walker Evans, Dorothea Lange, and others who had captured dust bowl refugees, migrant workers, and the rural poor of America. I never thought of myself as capable of creating such compelling images. I just wanted to be able to make practical photos, useful to movement organizers. But the Lange and Evans images were ever-present ghosts in the darkroom, challenging me to see differently. Under Matt's tutelage, honed by intensive shooting and long hours of printing, I came to love that moment when the image floated up through the developing solution.

At the age of one, Tamio Wakayama had been incarcerated in a cattle stockade along with his parents. Yes, the Canadian government, in a mirror of U.S. actions at the beginning of the Pacific war, had arrested all its citizens of Japanese ancestry, seized their property, and moved them to internment camps. Tamio grew up in such a camp, and like so many black children, came to believe that white was the coolest skin color of all. "I wanted desperately to be John Wayne," he told me, "but every time I looked in a mirror there was this fuckin' Jap staring back at me!" In Chatham, Ontario, where his parents began rebuilding their lives following the war, Tamio's playmates were mostly black. (Chatham had been a major terminus of the Underground Railway.) "It was us against all the rich kids."

Still later, during a break from college Tamio was watching lunch counter sit-ins on television, and saw black kids knocked off their seats get up and sit back at the counter again. "Given my background some part of me understood what they were going through. It was no wonder I identified with them." Thinking it might be a way to establish peace with his own demons, Wakayama decided to head south. He hooked up with SNCC in Birmingham right after the Klan bombing of the 16th Street Baptist Church, and soon was a volunteer working in SNCC's Atlanta office.

One day during SNCC's campaign to integrate Atlanta's downtown restaurants, he found himself alone in the office. Almost everybody else was in jail, but there was a pressing need to print up a flyer in support of further demonstrations. Wakayama found a photo in SNCC files of a Klansman in full regalia peering out through a restaurant window. "This is the face of Atlanta," his flyer read. "Let's change it." The result was so visually effective that photographer Danny Lyon began loaning Wakayama his cameras, encouraging him to develop his visual talent. "I considered Danny my mentor," Wakayama remembers, "and one of the first pictures I took with his camera was of a small boy flexing his muscles as two of them played Batman and Robin in the streets of Atlanta." But photography was not the only discovery Tamio made in Atlanta. Like so many of his black comrades, he began tracing a path back to the ethnic roots he had been taught as a child to despise. And Maria Varela was undergoing a similar transformation. I find it fascinating that they came south as "Tom" and "Mary," but left as Tamio and Maria.

Bobby Fletcher had taken a year off from grad school to work in the Harlem Education Project. One day he was photographing a street protest organized by some junkies who had been evicted from a local bar. He was grabbed by cops and thrown into a patrol car (New York police did not take kindly to photographers) where he found himself in a discussion as to whether he should be arrested. The discourse proceeded in an orderly manner until Fletcher blurted out: "A black man can't even take pictures in his own neighborhood!" That did it; he was arrested for disorderly conduct. The charges were later thrown out, but Fletcher reasoned that if he were going to be jailed, it might as well be for a worthy cause. He applied as a volunteer to the Mississippi Summer Project and spent the summer working and photographing in the black community of Harmony.

Although he was just getting started as a photographer, Fletcher carried compelling images of dust bowl poverty around in his head. In college at Fisk, his subscription to the *Saturday Review of Literature* had focused issue after issue on the documentary work of the Farm Security Administration as it pondered the question: was photography art? Fletcher devoured every page, but he also studied the Metropolitan Museum of Art's series of books on painting—all twenty-four volumes. "I can't draw," he told himself, "but I should be able to photograph."

Now in Mississippi he was anxious to create his own documentation. Sharecropping as a way of life was fast disappearing and Fletcher was determined to capture much of it before it was gone. In Tougaloo, a black suburb north of Jackson, he built a darkroom that was to serve the needs of the whole cadre of movement photographers. There he mastered filmstrip technology and worked with Maria Varela and Mary King to produce literacy slide shows and other organizing materials. In the fall of 1964 when many of us left the field, Fletcher, Wakayama, and Varela were among those who stayed on, shooting in and around SNCC projects until the movement as they knew it began to crumble away.

Bob Adelman was working in New York in the early sixties as a darkroom assistant at the *Reader's Digest*. "When the sit-ins started, it seemed to me the country was paralyzed as far as dealing with discrimination was concerned, but I saw the sit-ins as a way an average person could do something about an insoluble problem, so I volunteered with New York CORE." As a teenager, Adelman had had no contact at all with black people, but he loved jazz and used to sneak out at night to Birdland, one of New York's principal jazz clubs. "I didn't think of black people as oppressed, I thought of them as from some other planet, with this fantastic talent. Because I was Jewish, I had my own problems with discrimination, so I identified with black discrimination. My college thesis was on slave-breeding farms in the upper South."

Shooting for CORE, Adelman covered attempts to integrate eating establishments along Baltimore's Route 40. Eventually magazines began asking to see his contact sheets, and from this beginning Adelman gradually found his calling as a magazine photographer. He continued shooting for CORE in the Deep South, handling magazine assignments on the side and documenting life in remote black communities in Louisiana and Alabama. But he is best known for his incredible pictures of Birmingham police attempting to hose down demonstrators in Kelly Ingram Park.

For all of us, our cameras were vital tools—used hard and respected but not coddled. Those who could afford them shot with the gold standard of that era, the Nikon F. Not only was the "F" a superb single lens reflex camera; it also proved under hard usage to be extremely durable. More than once I dropped a camera while holding it over my head for a crowd shot and saw it bounce on the pavement at my feet. Usually I just picked it up and kept on shooting—I knew from experience that the "F" was hard to kill. If I ever did need a new body, I ordered it from Woods Photo Service in Hong Kong for $100–$125. (Try that today!) Whenever any of our cameras did succumb—to dust, humidity, hard usage, or inherent vice, we shipped these battered beauties off to Marty Forsher's Professional Camera

Repair in New York. Marty referred to them as "hockey pucks," and he fixed them up and mailed them back to us free of charge. Marty was one of the unsung heroes of the Civil Rights Movement. Since he serviced most of the top professionals in New York, he persuaded them to donate their used Pentax reflex cameras to the movement whenever they switched their studios to Nikons. These he repaired free and gave to us. Without Marty we might have been dead in the water.

We "learned" our cameras as extensions of our bodies. I taught myself to change film at a dead run, and after I discovered that a camera bag bouncing off my hip was more hindrance than help, I laced up a leather lens case with four compartments just wide enough to jam a lens into, and a fifth for film and filters. It fit the curve of my left hip, held there with belt loops, and with its flaps down I could take off at full gallop without shedding film or lenses. Bob Fitch referred to his cameras as "weapons" and, like any soldier, he taught himself to operate them seamlessly in the dark. He practiced setting speeds and apertures eyes closed, and learned to estimate exposures from experience—there was often no time to read a light meter. From the photojournalist Charlie Moore, I learned to shoot action right on top of it, working almost in the middle with a 24mm wide angle lens. Standing back with a telephoto might be safer but the pictures were no good—they lacked a sense of immediacy and dramatic motion. Besides, I discovered that when the action was really hot the protagonists were barely aware of one's presence—so focused were they on the drama at hand. Move fast and keep shooting—that was my mantra.

Most of us had our personal strategies for staying safe while staying in action. But one overriding principle governed us all: our job was to get the pictures and get them out into the wider world, not to collect glory or jail time as some civil rights hero. As photographers we worked fully exposed and if we got arrested and/or lost our film, we had failed at our job. Consequently, any tactic or ruse that kept us going, no matter how cowardly, was perfectly acceptable. On occasion we lied, used fake press credentials, toadied up to police,

or pretended to be someone else—all in the service of our cause. Mostly, we never admitted we were working for or with the movement. Simply being there was tough enough.

Bob Adelman is a big man and a charming one, and he often used his charm on the Powers That Be. He remembers shooting in Sumter, South Carolina, during a CORE voter registration drive.

When I wasn't busy I would wander around town taking pictures. A city official asked me what I was doing. I told him I was a service man from the nearby air force base and had pleasant memories of the town, so I was taking some pictures for memory's sake. He was so won over that he took me on a personal tour of the town. In the courthouse I saw blacks lined up to register and I asked him, "Do those people actually vote here?"

I had the reputation in the movement of being rather fearless. I thought I was doing the right thing and that I had a right to photograph. It was probably a stupid idea, but that was the way I felt. I was routinely arrested. They'd feed you some turnips and when the demonstration was over, they'd let you go. I wasn't bound by nonviolence because I wasn't a demonstrator, so occasionally I would use my Leica as a weapon, whipping it around when I felt threatened. Toward the end of 1965 driving through Mississippi and Louisiana I got so paranoid I carried a gun in my car. And everywhere I went both blacks and whites had guns.

Bob Fitch lacked the luxury of subterfuge.

I had no credentials. They would be no good to me. Everyone knew who I was and who I was working for. I got a lot of harassment, a lot of traffic tickets. I kept a fifty-dollar bill in my shoe to pay the tickets. Often it was very gamy—the cops would get a chuckle out of it.

But not always.

In Greenville, Alabama, I was covering a march to the courthouse of kids who were demonstrating so their

parents could vote. That night as we left town we were stopped by the local sheriff, who pulled me out of my car and put me in the sheriff's car. We ended up in his office with him holding a Saturday night special to my head, cocked and loaded. I could see the bullets in the gun—it was only a few inches from my eyeballs, but what really scared me was how hard his hand was shaking— I was afraid the gun would go off. I prayed, but not to God. I prayed to Carl Rodgers, the father of nondirective therapy. I'd learned to apply this in tight situations, reflecting back to a person what they were saying and feeling. I said to the sheriff, "You hate my guts, and you want to see me dead!" And he screamed at me, "You're goddamned right I do," plus a lot of stuff he was feeling about the racial situation. He knew everything about me. He'd read the Alabama Bureau of Investigation file on me. After quite a long stretch and a lot of venting of this stuff, he took a deep breath, dropped the gun and uncocked the trigger, saying, "Get the fuck out of my town." That gave me a little confidence, and I asked him, "Am I going to get out of this town alive?" He said, "Yes, you'll get out of the town," which made me wonder what would happen after I left the town. Instead I found the black ghetto and spent the night at a Freedom House.

Maria Varela reflected on how developing the street smarts to survive became the new "normal" in our nonnormal lives.

Terrifying encounters became "normal" to those of us working in the movement who were new to the South. They had been "normal" for generations for those born and raised under southern U.S. apartheid. As civil rights workers, we had to be prepared anytime, anywhere to walk the killing fields. We learned a variety of responses to danger: sometimes to fade into the background, assuming local accent and dress, sometimes to emotionally play dead in hopes the stalker would lose interest or sometimes to do something so bold as to catch him off balance, enabling flight. We learned how to overcome the paralysis of fear and developed finely tuned survival senses we never knew we had.

But for most of us, the fear never left. After my family moved to New Orleans in the fall of 1964, I required a full two years before I was able to shake the habit of constantly watching my rearview mirror whenever I drove somewhere to check who might be following me. Driving anywhere was always fear-filled. As Bob Fitch recalls:

I remember driving back to California one time, going through Needles in Southern California, and suddenly seeing a cop car following behind me. I checked my speed and drove very carefully. Then the highway patrol pulled around me and went on its way, and I broke into weeping—weeping so hard I had to pull off the road. I wept because I was in California and didn't have to be afraid. The cloud of terror was just part of the environment. We lived within it and just had to put it aside to get the work done. I'd go to church in Atlanta to hear Dr. King preach, but when the choir started up, I'd begin to weep because in that church I was safe.

We all had our stories, but this one from Maria Varela stays with me.

Swing Down, Sweet Chariot, and Let Me Ride
I looked down at the speedometer. It hovered at 115. My 1957 Packard hunkered down and propelled the three of us down Mississippi Interstate 55. Glancing to the side I saw the two-toned '67 Chevy with its white occupants trying to pass us . . . yet again. The barrel of a long gun poked up between the two men in the front seat.

It seemed like an eternity since we had left Memphis and got on the interstate. Earlier that day, my companions, an older black woman and her daughter, and I had left a SNCC gathering at Highlander Center in Tennessee. We were on our way to the Mississippi Delta. Traveling in an integrated car in daylight had left us all a little tense. When we stopped for gas in Memphis that evening, I thought that the cover of darkness meant the worst of the journey was over. Then I turned from the gas pump and saw the white male occupants of the Chevy staring at us. It was the fall of 1964: open season on civil rights workers.

The Packard moved effortlessly up to 120 mph. It ran as if made for this speed: not a shake or shimmy. My companions were deathly quiet. I closed my mind to thoughts of danger: gunfire from the pursuing car, a collision, a flat tire, a blown rod, or what would happen if the Chevy managed to pull in front and stop us. It was a moonless night and my eyes were glued to the black strip of asphalt which stretched before us. One thing I knew for sure—I would sooner risk pushing the car to the end of the speedometer than stop on this desolate stretch of road in the far northern reaches of Mississippi.

Up ahead we saw a semitruck. The lack of any traffic since Memphis had made the pursuit lethal. If I could stay with the semi perhaps the pursuers wouldn't make their move. We were now at 125 shooting down the road trying to catch up to the tractor-trailer. As I pulled alongside the truck, the Chevy was on our tail. It was a delicate maneuver, slowing the Packard enough to allow me to slip in front of the semi, yet going fast enough to shake off the Chevy. Once in front, the trick was to stay close to the semi so the Chevy could not come in between. The truck slowed way down and so did we.

Then the trucker tried to pass us. I sped up, staying as close to his front bumper as I dared. The Chevy tried unsuccessfully to move ahead of us both, but finally fell back behind the semi. We hovered close to our "guardian" semi for another few miles. The panic welling in my throat was held at bay by my companions' silent composure. Signs to the Batesville exit emerged. I shot back up to 125. I made the exit with neither truck nor Chevy in sight, cut the lights and floated down the exit ramp into welcome darkness. The semi and the Chevy roared over us into the night. There was not a word spoken as we continued through Batesville on our way down to the Delta. The terror gradually subsided. Finally in small murmurs, with a few tenuous chuckles, we dared to believe it was over. I thought that the Packard Company must have been God's chariot maker. ["Swing Down, Sweet Chariot, and Let Me Ride" is reprinted with permission from Maria Varela's essay in *Hands on the Freedom Plow: Personal Accounts by Women in SNCC*, ed. Faith Holsaert et al., University of Illinois Press.]

Considering the environment in whch we worked, it's a wonder we could make pictures at all—fear is supposed to be a paralyzing emotion. But we were not paralyzed, perhaps because social commitment is stronger than fear. The photographs that follow speak of this.

The Photographs

Text by Charles E. Cobb, Jr.

Part One: **Black Life**

Grassroots organizing across the "Black Belt" best describes the 1960s Southern Freedom Movement. It was dangerous work punctuated by murder. The Black Belt curves through hundreds of counties from Maryland to Texas. In many, black people are a majority. It still contains some of America's poorest counties, like Quitman County in Mississippi where a third of the population lives below the poverty line. In the 1960s the county's average annual per family income was only one thousand dollars.

Rev. Ralph David Abernathy, Martin Luther King's good friend and SCLC associate, tells of a 1966 visit they made to a school there. A teacher they were visiting needed to feed her students and excused herself: "It's lunchtime," she explained.

"We watched as she brought out a box of crackers and a brown bag filled with apples; then she went around to each desk and gave each child a stack of four or five crackers and a quarter of an apple.

"'That's all they get,' I whispered."

King turned to his friend, nodding his head. "And I saw that his eyes were full of tears."

Everywhere, black life was harsh and disempowered. And everywhere, oppressive laws imposed racial discrimination and segregation. Violence was regularly used to enforce white supremacy.

Nonetheless, deprivation, terror, and fear did not begin to describe or define black community life. There was love and laughter and play and family and strength and pride; and most significantly, against all odds, determination to make life better. These communities were the heartland of the Southern Freedom Movement.

Strength where you might least expect it was often encountered—as in the face of this rural Alabama man—reflecting vitality and dignity in a society trying to strip it away.

Bob Fitch, Alabama, 1965

LEFT A Mississippi Delta farmer shows photographer Tamio Wakayama internal organs that will be his family's dinner. "I had the feeling," Wakayama recalled, "of lives blending seamlessly with the black soil of the cotton fields, creating a visual and organic unity."

Tamio Wakayama, Mississippi Delta, 1964

BELOW Children improvise a playground in the Child Development Group of Mississippi, one of the nation's first Head Start programs.

Bob Fletcher, Mississippi, 1965

BELOW Resourcefulness was essential for survival in the cash-poor communities of the Black Belt— vegetable gardens, hogs rooting in the yard, or fish from a nearby pond provided food for the table.

Bob Fletcher, Mississippi Delta, 1965

RIGHT Laughter, often loud and generous like that coming from this rural Alabama woman on her front porch, punctuated everyday life.

Bob Fitch, Alabama, 1965

BELOW Youthful energy, as with this boy proudly demonstrating his vigor on the streets of Atlanta, was not crushed by segregation's viciousness.

Tamio Wakayama, Atlanta, Georgia, 1963

RIGHT The sister of this woman died when her Birmingham house burned due to late arrival of the fire department. Black neighborhoods were notoriously neglected.

Bob Fitch, Birmingham, Alabama, 1965

LEFT The carefully lettered sign supports a boycott of merchants who refused to hire blacks in the small town of Grenada, Mississippi, where half the population was black.

Bob Fitch, Grenada, Mississippi, 1966

BELOW In 1965, a small, defiant group of sharecroppers began demanding a fair wage and went on strike, giving birth to the Mississippi Freedom Labor Union.

Bob Fletcher, Mississippi Delta, 1965

LEFT Alabama man shows a head wound he received from a beating by the Klan.

Bob Fitch, Alabama, 1965

BELOW "More than poverty," explained the photographer, "I saw harmony between the sharecropper's shack, the outhouse, and the black soil. It began my long love affair with that land and its people."

Tamio Wakayama, Mississippi Delta, 1964

Photographer Maria Varela recalled: "We organized, traveling winter-ravaged country roads, going house to house, and sometimes no one would open the door."

Maria Varela, Rosedale, Mississippi, 1966

Blues fertilized Delta life. Jamie Sims, blind from birth and subject to a poverty that left him few options, spent much of his life on his front porch, playing guitar.

Matt Herron, Valley View, Mississippi, 1964

LEFT The Child Development Group of Mississippi (CDGM) was one of the nation's first Head Start programs. Here at a CDGM site in Leake County's Harmony community, a child practices writing her letters.

Bob Fletcher, Harmony, Mississippi, 1965

ABOVE This black elementary school typifies Alabama's "separate but equal" school system.

Matt Herron, Lowndes County, Alabama, 1965

ABOVE This home is typical of plantation housing.

Maria Varela, Rosedale, Mississippi, 1966

RIGHT "The children wanted to know," photographer Maria Varela remembers, "What was I doing here? Where was I from? Was I a 'Freedom Rider'? They lived life front and center on their faces."

Maria Varela, Rosedale, Mississippi, 1966

BELOW A sharecropper shack in Itta Bena, Mississippi, and a vanishing way of life. Despite great poverty, love and care made a home and informed black life across the Delta.

Bob Fletcher, Mississippi Delta, 1965

RIGHT George Reed stands in front of a mule at St. Paul's Missionary Baptist Church.

Matt Herron, Valley View, Mississippi, 1964

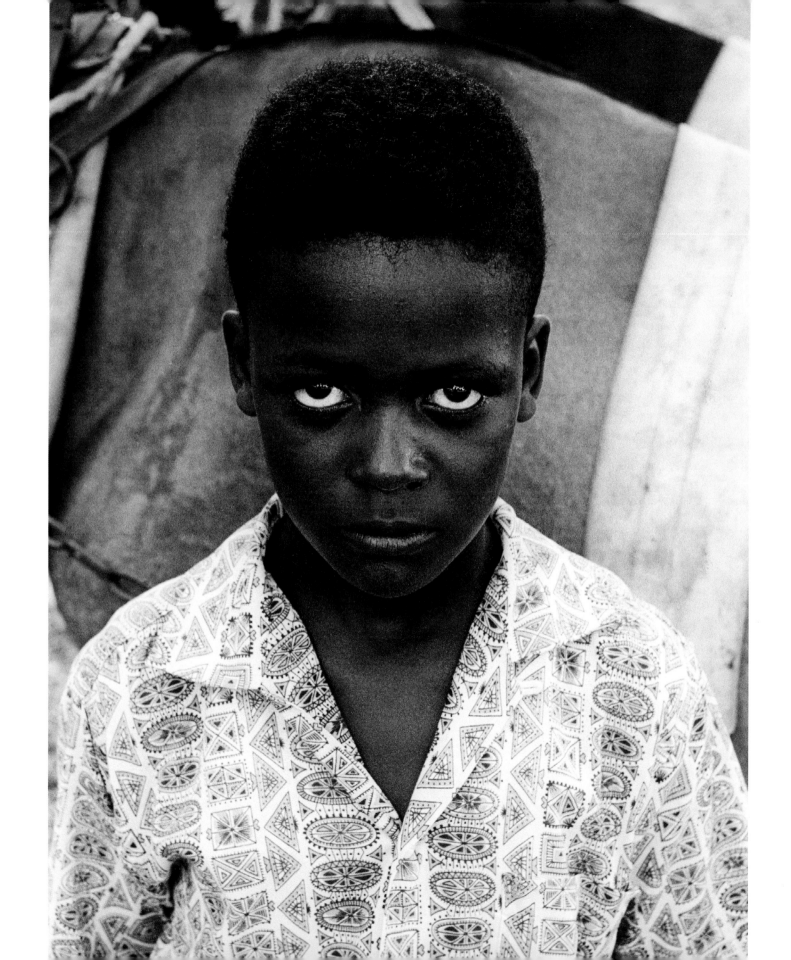

LEFT For Rev. McCraney and his wife, like many rural Mississippi people, burial insurance, enabling a dignified funeral, was the final antidote to poverty.

Bob Fletcher, Mississippi Delta, 1965

ABOVE "Everywhere I traveled in the rural South," the photographer remembered, "whether in Mississippi, Alabama, or Georgia, the general store served as a daily gathering place for the older men."

Bob Fletcher, Leflore County, Mississippi, 1965

ABOVE In their Sunday best, young men and boys
stand in a glade behind the church.

Matt Herron, Valley View, Mississippi, 1964

RIGHT At St. Paul's Missionary Baptist Church,
men gather before the service.

Matt Herron, Valley View, Mississippi, 1964

BELOW St. Paul's congregation of sharecroppers could not afford a fulltime minister. Rev. Percy Gordon, a circuit preacher, conducted service every fourth Sunday.

Matt Herron, Valley View, Mississippi, 1964

RIGHT The congregation gathered in its Sunday best. Some parishioners walked the dusty roads to church barefoot, carrying their shoes, so they would be spotless for service. It was a way of respecting themselves in a society that gave them no respect.

Matt Herron, Valley View, Mississippi, 1964

ABOVE Cotton pickers earned three dollars a day. This backbreaking labor was being rapidly mechanized in the 1960s, and income for field workers was vanishing.

Bob Fletcher, Mississippi Delta, 1965

RIGHT Black labor maintained white privilege. In Jackson, Mississippi, a gardener trims the front yard of an award-winning lawn.

Matt Herron, Jackson, Mississippi, 1963

ABOVE At this socialite gathering in Dallas, the maid was just another piece of the furniture.

Bob Adelman, Dallas, Texas, 1964

RIGHT This woman stands ready at the county courthouse on a Greewood, Mississippi, "Freedom Day." Scores lined up to register to vote. Police arrested many and hauled them to jail in a city bus.

Bob Fletcher, Greenwood, Mississippi, 1964

ABOVE Proud of the meals from her wood-burning stove, Mrs. Maggie Lee Pettway also was proud of her wallpaper, and proud of Martin Luther King, "who got us to the place where we wasn't afraid. We needed someone to stand for us who wasn't afraid."

Bob Adelman, Camden, Alabama, 1966

RIGHT This man is breaking the law at this courthouse.

Bob Adelman, Clinton, Louisiana, 1964

Part Two: **Organizing for Freedom**

Community leaders, many of whom were World War II veterans and led NAACP branches, encouraged SNCC to make voting rights a priority. White-black population ratios indicated that gaining the right to vote would cause a dramatic and beneficial shift of power relations at state and local levels. Thus, from an organization of sit-in students, SNCC became an organization of organizers with more full-time field secretaries than any of the older civil rights groups. SNCC's approach was "radical," but what made it radical was the people SNCC worked with. Most were people whose voices were usually unheard or ignored—like Mrs. Fannie Lou Hamer, a sharecropper, who after attempting to register to vote returned to the plantation where she picked cotton and refused the plantation owner's demand that she make no further attempts. "I didn't go down there to register for you," she told him. "I went to register for myself." He immediately threw her off the plantation. Soon, however, the forty-six-year-old Mrs. Hamer was one of the Mississippi movement's most powerful voices and SNCC's oldest field secretary.

Increasingly, though, whites reacted to voter registration efforts with greater violence. The Ku Klux Klan expanded across the state. Early in 1963, a machine gun ambush outside the city of Greenwood almost killed SNCC worker Jimmy Travis when three of the bullets slammed into his upper body. On June 12, 1963, Mississippi NAACP field secretary Medgar Evers was murdered by an assassin who shot him from a hiding place in the bushes across the street from Evers's home. Additionally, whole communities were punished with economic reprisal or denial of welfare assistance when any resident attempted to register to vote.

A "mock" vote is held to demonstrate that blacks desire to vote. The woman on the left, Ida Mae Holland, was a prostitute before joining the movement. She later attended college, earned a PhD, and became a playwright.

Matt Herron, Greenwood, Mississippi, 1963

LEFT A passerby cautiously looks at civil rights literature in a Freedom House window. Involvement in the movement often led to the loss of a job and other retaliation by local whites.

Tamio Wakayama, Mound Bayou, Mississippi, 1964

ABOVE After the Ku Klux Klan burned this cross in front of a Mississippi Delta Freedom House, a civil rights worker transformed it with a painted message.

Tamio Wakayama, Indianola, Mississippi, 1964

In the Greenwood COFO office, project director Sam
Block is making assignments. In February 1963,
segregationists firebombed the Greenwood office, and
SNCC worker Jimmy Travis was machine-gunned on
the highway just outside town.

Matt Herron, Greenwood, Mississippi, 1963

Most of America ignored the mounting terror, and the federal government said it could not offer protection, so COFO—the Council of Federated Organizations, a statewide coalition of local groups that SNCC and other national civil rights organizations staffed—decided to bring the nation's children to Mississippi. Almost one thousand student volunteers were recruited for a 1964 "Freedom Summer." Although getting national attention was urgent, COFO organizers worried about the effect of bringing such a large number of untrained and untested, mostly northern, white student volunteers into Mississippi. In fact, most opposed the idea. However, almost all of the community leaders around the state— grassroots "local people" like Mrs. Hamer—strongly favored summer volunteers coming to Mississippi. In their experience, people coming from the outside—whether from another part of Mississippi or from New York City—were a good thing. It meant they were not alone. It increased pressure on unchecked white power. And though racial integration was against the law in Mississippi, local people made it plain that they would integrate these volunteers into black community life. White students would sleep in their homes; eat at their tables; socialize in their dirt yards; and go to their churches on Sundays. COFO workers deferred to this community disposition—for a basic principle underlying COFO's organizing work was that people should gain control of the decision-making affecting their lives. Therefore, despite misgivings, it was impossible, in fact contradictory, to say, "We don't like your decision so we won't work with you." After a brief period of orientation and training at the Western College for Women in Oxford, Ohio, the volunteers came to Mississippi.

LEFT Summer volunteer Peter Werner tries to explain to family members that earlier in the day he was attacked while leaving a Walgreen store, and after the assault, local police arrested him and charged him with assault.

Herbert Randall, Hattiesburg, Mississippi, 1964

ABOVE While introducing himself to business owners along Hattiesburg's Mobile Street, Sandy Leigh, project director for COFO, takes a break at Jean Connor's Beauty Shop.

Herbert Randall, Hattiesburg, Mississippi, 1964

LEFT This is the scene inside COFO's Jackson, Mississippi headquarters on Lynch Street, before the MFDP delegation leaves for the Atlantic City Democratic National Convention. Mary King, assistant to SNCC's communications director, Julian Bond, is on the phone, informing the media.

George Ballis, Jackson, Mississippi, 1964

ABOVE This unattributed photo of an Oxford, Ohio, demonstration was found amongst the images Herbert Randall took in June 1964.

Unknown photographer, Western College for Women, Oxford, Ohio, 1964

At the Oxford, Ohio, training and orientation session,
summer volunteers gather after learning that three
civil rights workers are missing and presumed dead
in Mississippi.

**Herbert Randall, Western College for Women, Oxford,
Ohio, 1964**

During orientation and training for the 1964
Mississippi Summer Project, volunteers learn to
protect themselves nonviolently from assault.

**Herbert Randall, Western College for Women, Oxford,
Ohio, 1964**

ABOVE At the end of their training week, volunteers join hands and sing "We Shall Overcome" before boarding a bus bound for Mississippi.

Tamio Wakayama, Western College for Women, Oxford, Ohio, 1964

RIGHT The probable fate of three missing civil rights workers weighs heavily on the minds of volunteers as they prepare to board a bus for Mississippi.

Tamio Wakayama, Western College for Women, Oxford, Ohio, 1964

Edie Black from Smith College bonds with Freedom
School students in Mileston. Most of the students
had never imagined the possibility of friendship
with a white person. Their lives and the lives of the
volunteers were changed forever.

Matt Herron, Mileston, Mississippi, 1964

At the Mileston Freedom School, a summer volunteer
teaches a science class outdoors.

Matt Herron, Mileston, Mississippi, 1964

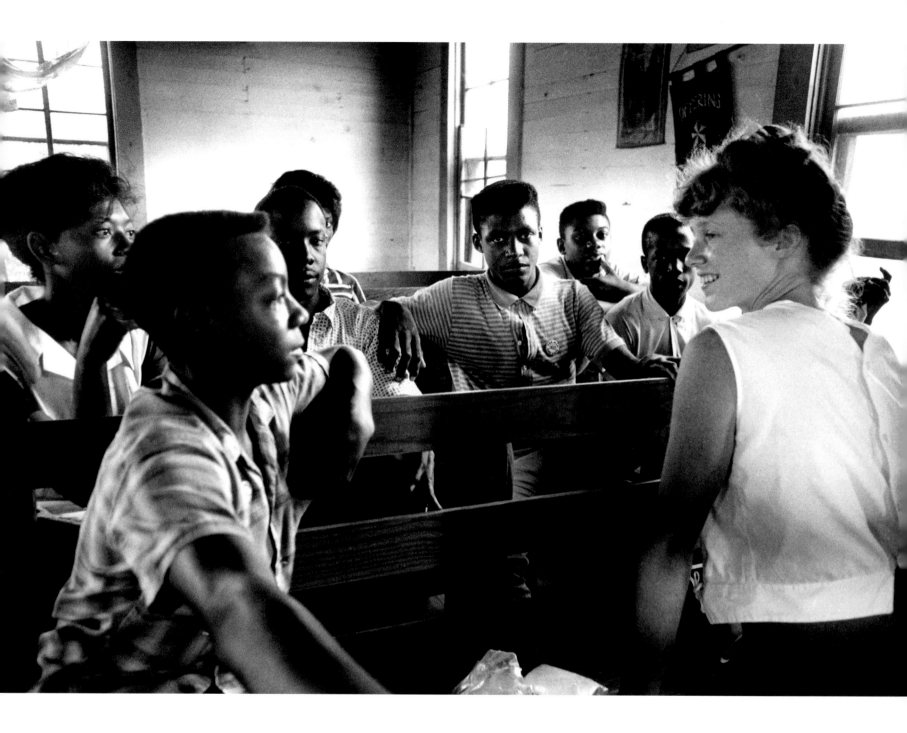

ABOVE Freedom School student Eddie Carthan (front row, left) grew up to become mayor of Tchula, a town near Mileston. His efforts to transform the town threatened local white planters who had him jailed on a trumped-up murder charge.

Matt Herron, Mileston, Mississippi, 1964

RIGHT Summer volunteer Mario Savio takes a bath behind the Mileston Freedom House. After returning to the University of California at Berkeley, Savio organized the Free Speech Movement. Its protests spread to colleges and universities across the nation.

Matt Herron, Mileston, Mississippi, 1964

The movement was nonviolent; the community was not. Summer volunteer Jim Boebel and a resident armed with a shotgun guard the newly constructed Freedom School library after a bomb threat by local whites.

Matt Herron, Mileston, Mississippi, 1964

Wondering if barriers in her young life would ever come down, sixteen-year-old Gracie Hawthorne sits outside of COFO headquarters at 507 Mobile Street and gazes toward the railroad crossing that separates white and black Hattiesburg.

Herbert Randall, Hattiesburg, Mississippi, 1964

NOTICE
Applications for Registration must
be completely filled out without any
assistance or suggestions of any
person or memorandum.
After 10 days applicant's names and
addresses are published for two consecutive
weeks in the newspaper. They cannot be
ruled on until 14days after the second
ublication. Therefore it can take as long as
3days before we can give you an answer
as to your application being accepted
or rejected.
Your indulgence is appreciated.
The REGISTRAR

Black citizens fill out voter registration forms at the Forrest County Courthouse. The sign on the wall illustrates the ordeal of public exposure applicants faced, a tactic used to discourage black registration. Applicants could lose jobs or have their houses firebombed after their names were published in the local newspaper.

Matt Herron, Hattiesburg, Mississippi, 1964

Summer volunteer Jim Nance begins another day of
door-to-door canvassing in a black neighborhood in
Hattiesburg. He'll try to persuade residents to register
to vote at the county courthouse.

Herbert Randall, Hattiesburg, Mississippi, 1964

Conversation was COFO's main tool. Volunteer Dick Landerman talks to Hattie Mae Pough, promising his assistance and urging her to accompany him to the voter registration office.

Herbert Randall, Hattiesburg, Mississippi, 1964

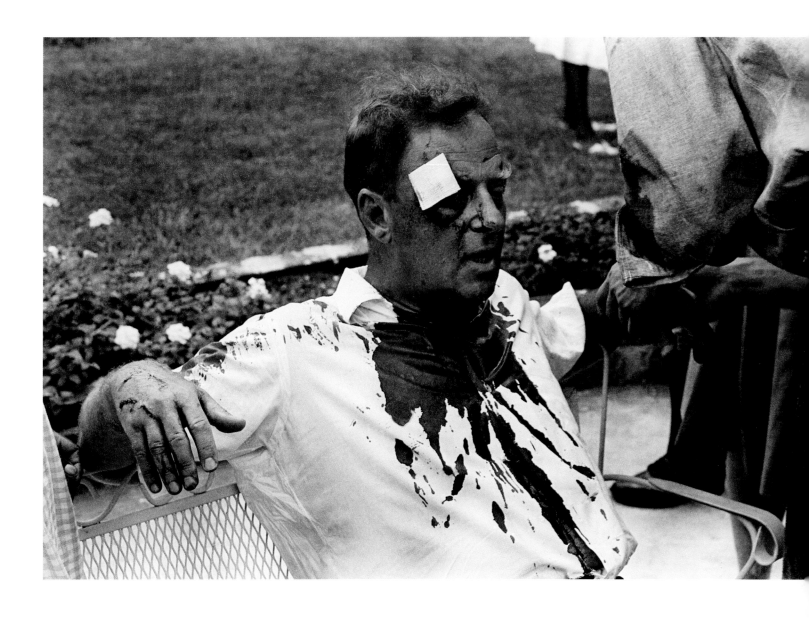

White volunteers did not escape assault. Arthur Lelyveld, a rabbi from Cleveland, Ohio, receives first aid after being beaten with a tire iron.

Herbert Randall, Hattiesburg, Mississippi, 1964

A study in patient impatience, voter applicants line up
then wait and wait and wait to register.

Bob Adelman, Clinton, Louisiana, 1964

Local white farmers gather menacingly outside a voter registration office where blacks are attempting to register. Potential black registrants often encountered this scene at county courthouses.

Tamio Wakayama, Southwest Georgia, 1963

A black citizen fills out a registration form under the watchful—and not especially friendly—eye of the local registrar.

Tamio Wakayama, Southwest Georgia, 1963

In April 1964 the Mississippi Freedom Democratic Party was created and began preparing to challenge the all-white Mississippi Democratic Party's legitimacy at the national party convention in August. Surprisingly progressive rules governing delegate selection mandated a transparent and democratic process; but secret meetings, men standing in doorways physically barring entrance to meetings, last-minute changes of meeting times and places, and other methods deliberately violated those rules in order to prevent black participation. The first step of the MFDP challenge was to systematically test and confirm black exclusion. Precinct meetings began the process of delegate selection, and in Clarksdale when Aaron Henry, the NAACP state president as well as president of COFO, brought a group of twenty blacks to a precinct meeting, they greatly outnumbered the seven whites there. The surprised chair delayed the meeting until enough whites to outnumber Henry's group were rounded up. A few days later, one of those whites *thanked* Henry. "I'm sure glad y'all went down there. . . . They never let us get involved before, but when y'all showed up, they called us and let us have something to say at last." By following delegate selection rules exactly, and documenting discrimination by the official state party, the MFDP believed it would have a strong, provable basis for recognition as the legitimate state party at the national convention. Over the summer, great effort went into organizing the required precinct, county, and district meetings that culminated in a state convention in Jackson where a sixty-eight-person MFDP delegation for the national convention was selected.

Inside the Atlantic City Convention Hall, MFDP delegate Fannie Lou Hamer and COFO leader Bob Moses assess the Mississippi seating situation.

George Ballis, Atlantic City, New Jersey, 1964

Rev. Martin Luther King testifies before a
subcommittee of the Democratic Party Credentials
Committee as to why MFDP delegates should be
seated at the convention: "I say to you that any party
in the world should be proud to have a delegation such
as this seated in their midst." Minnesota attorney
general Walter Mondale (center), Senator Hubert
Humphrey's protégé, chaired this subcommittee. Word
had "quickly spread" in the convention that Humphrey
would be chosen as President Johnson's running mate
if the subcommittee succeeded in "handling," i.e.,
disarming, the MFDP challenge.

George Ballis, Atlantic City, New Jersey, 1964

ABOVE MFDP delegates demonstrate as President Lyndon Johnson is being nominated. Victoria Gray from Hattiesburg, the woman at center, is a prominent MFDP leader.

George Ballis, Atlantic City, New Jersey, 1964

RIGHT With borrowed ID's from friendly delegates, MFDP supporters demonstrate on the convention floor. Their "One Man One Vote" banners are quickly ripped in the turmoil created by Johnson-Humphrey supporters.

George Ballis, Atlantic City, New Jersey, 1964

LEFT MFDP demonstrators seek to assert their presence on the convention floor.

George Ballis, Atlantic City, New Jersey, 1964

ABOVE Ella Baker addresses MFDP delegates at a boardwalk rally during the convention. The portrait in the background is of Michael "Mickey" Schwerner, one of three civil rights workers murdered at the start of Freedom Summer.

George Ballis, Atlantic City, New Jersey, 1964

MFDP demonstrations continued on the Atlantic City boardwalk day and night. Supporters here hold a casket to memorialize civil rights workers James Earl Chaney, Michael "Mickey" Schwerner, and Andrew Goodman, who were murdered by Klansmen.

George Ballis, Atlantic City, New Jersey, 1964

A fireworks display flares up on the Atlantic City
boardwalk to memorialize the murdered civil rights
workers.

George Ballis, Atlantic City, New Jersey, 1964

Fannie Lou Hamer reacts angrily to the unfair compromise offered MFDP delegates seeking to be seated at the Democratic National Convention—"We didn't come all this way for no two seats!"

George Ballis, Atlantic City, New Jersey, 1964

Of all the black establishment leaders, Rev. Martin Luther King gave the MFDP the greatest support. Though he was not walking down dirt roads as a denim-clad community organizer, and was representing what for many in the field was the top-down patriarchal tradition of black pastors, understanding the southern movement requires appreciation of Rev. King. His identification with protests in Montgomery, Alabama, and later Birmingham, inspired struggle for civil rights because it symbolized the possibility of victory. He had an easy southern warmth with people he encountered. He liked SNCC's young people. and maybe even saw a little of himself in them, for he was just twenty-six years old in 1955 when he emerged as the leader of the Montgomery bus boycott. "What is new in your fight," King admiringly told a Durham, North Carolina, audience shortly after sit-ins erupted, "is the fact that it was initiated, fed, and sustained by students." Ella Baker had successfully obtained funds from Rev. King to bring sit-in leaders together at Shaw College, because he hoped that they would form a youth arm of SCLC. The students, however, insisted on forming their own organization. And though the press often played up disagreements between SNCC and SCLC, there was a great deal of interaction and cooperation between them. SNCC organizers liked King even though they disagreed with the leader-centered style of his organization of black preachers. But even in teasing Rev. King, as when calling him "de Lawd," they understood the stature he had with black people in the South.

LEFT Rev. Martin Luther King stands in his Atlanta office. Wall portrait is of Mohandas Gandhi, whose discipline of nonviolent resistance to evil King adopted.

Bob Fitch, Atlanta, Georgia, 1966

ABOVE Rev. Martin Luther King plays pool with kids during a tour of a Chicago neighborhood.

Bob Fitch, Chicago, Illinois, 1966

ABOVE Rev. Martin Luther King preaches to an overflow crowd at a mass civil rights meeting.

Bob Fitch, Eutaw, Alabama, 1965

RIGHT Rev. Martin Luther King leads children who are integrating a Grenada, Mississippi, school. Behind him are Andrew Young, carrying a child, and Hosea Williams. Behind Young is folksinger Joan Baez, whose contributions financed the Grenada campaign.

Bob Fitch, Grenada, Mississippi, 1966

ABOVE At a Kelly Ingram Park rally, Rev. Martin Luther King sits with his children, Martin III and Yolanda. Unseen here but across the street is the 16th Street Baptist Church where four young girls were killed by a Klan bomb in 1963.

Bob Fitch, Kelly Ingram Park, Birmingham, Alabama, 1965

RIGHT Not everything was grim. Birmingham leader Rev. Fred Shuttlesworth and Rev. Martin Luther King share a joke during SCLC's "People-To-People" tour.

Bob Fitch, Kelly Ingram Park, Birmingham, Alabama, 1965

LEFT On-the-spot meetings were common. (Left to right) Rev. Fred Shuttlesworth, Bernard Lee, Rev. Martin Luther King, and Hosea Williams confer during a rally in Kelly Ingram Park.

Bob Fitch, Kelly Ingram Park, Birmingham, Alabama, 1965

ABOVE A weary Rev. Martin Luther King relaxes at the Montgomery airport with his SCLC lieutenant Andrew Young.

Bob Fitch, Montgomery, Alabama, 1966

The march that began in Selma, Alabama, March 21, 1965, culminating four days later in the state's capital city, Montgomery, was a tipping point. The marchers were predominantly Alabamians from Selma and the surrounding counties, but numerous participants came from across the United States. Some were prominent, like Nobel Prize winner Dr. Ralph Bunche; others were more ordinary: clergy, blue- and white-collar workers, students. All shared the belief that America could no longer postpone redeeming what at the 1963 March on Washington Martin Luther King had characterized as a "promissory note" in default, signed by America's architects. This note "was a promise that all men would be guaranteed the inalienable rights of life, liberty, and the pursuit of happiness." The specific issue defining the march was the wall of resistance to voter registration efforts. Between January and March 1965, more than three thousand people had been arrested in the voter registration campaign organized by SNCC and SCLC. Tragically, however, a killing had forced the issue. In nearby Perry County, where SCLC had also mounted a voter registration drive, police gunned down one of the local participants, Jimmie Lee Jackson. An attempted march to Montgomery on March 7, protesting both Jackson's murder and the denial of voting rights, was savagely halted by state police and a sheriff's posse that first fired tear gas as marchers knelt to pray, then waded into the marchers clubbing them with nightsticks. An appalled nation witnessed this police riot on television. March 7, 1965, a Sunday, became, and is still known as, "Bloody Sunday."

March leaders (wearing leis) prepare to leave Selma at the start of the third march. (Left to right) John Lewis, a nun, Rev. Ralph Abernathy, Rev. Martin Luther King, Ralph Bunche, and Rabbi Abraham Joshua Heschel.

Matt Herron, Selma, Alabama, 1965

LEFT Rev. Martin Luther King leads singing marchers toward Montgomery. In the front row (on the right) is SNCC chairman John Lewis.

Matt Herron, Selma-Montgomery, Alabama, 1965

ABOVE Selma marchers pass lines of United States troops. Alabama governor George Wallace refused to offer protection to the march, so President Lyndon Johnson nationalized the Alabama National Guard.

Matt Herron, Selma–Montgomery, Alabama, 1965

ABOVE Selma marchers enter Montgomery in a rainstorm.

Matt Herron, Montgomery, Alabama, 1965

RIGHT Though too young to vote, Bobby Simmons proclaims his convictions on his forehead. After he walked all the way to Montgomery, Bobby said, "You be rejoicing once you accomplish your goal and get there."

Matt Herron, Selma–Montgomery, Alabama, 1965

LEFT Despite having only one leg, Jim Leatherer walked the entire fifty miles on crutches.

Matt Herron, Selma–Montgomery, Alabama, 1965

ABOVE Doris Wilson's feet need help early in the Selma march. Her shoes are nearly gone.

Matt Herron, Selma–Montgomery, Alabama, 1965

LEFT "I'm walking for my freedom!" exclaimed twenty-year-old Doris Wilson of Selma. She was fired from her twelve-dollar-a-week job in a school lunchroom for taking part in voter registration efforts, and her father was removed from welfare rolls.

Matt Herron, Selma–Montgomery, Alabama, 1965

ABOVE At the end of a day's walk, marchers sing a freedom song: "Ya Gotta Do Like the Spirit Say Do."

Matt Herron, Selma–Montgomery, Alabama, 1965

ABOVE An Alabama farmer in his work clothes joins the march.

Matt Herron, Lowndes County, Alabama, 1965

RIGHT For many black residents of Lowndes County, the sight of thousands of blacks and whites walking unmolested through one of Alabama's most virulently racist counties was a vision they never expected to behold.

Matt Herron, Lowndes County, Alabama, 1965

The Voting Rights Act signed into law by President Lyndon Johnson on August 6, 1965, outlawed discriminatory standards, practices, and procedures in voting and voter registration. It also provided for federal oversight in states with a history of voting discrimination. Mississippi's freedom struggle had played a major role in getting this legislation on the congressional agenda. Selma's dramatic events gave a final nudge to passage. The act's significance was almost immediately felt in notorious Lowndes County where 80 percent of county residents were black, yet not a single black person was registered to vote. Most of the land between Selma and Montgomery is Lowndes County, and, in the wake of the march, SNCC's Stokely Carmichael and a small band of organizers began digging in there. The county's fearsome reputation for antiblack terror had resulted in the nickname "Bloody Lowndes," but a small core of independent black farmers had for decades been challenging the white power that ruled county life. There were "strong people we could work with," said Stokely Carmichael about the decision to begin organizing there. In April 1966, under state law, the Lowndes County Freedom Organization (LCFO) registered as a political party. It is one of SNCC's least-known success stories. By the time LCFO was organized, black registered voters outnumbered white registered voters in Lowndes County. LCFO's symbol was a black panther. That same year, two young men organizing in Oakland, California—Huey P. Newton and Bobby Seale—asked SNCC if they could use the symbol. Though the militant party they organized gained national fame, it was the *second* Black Panther Party.

Septima Clark, whose "Citizenship Schools" across the South linked reading-and-writing literacy with political literacy, helps a prospective voter learn to read and write.

Bob Fitch, Camden, Alabama, 1966

LEFT El Fondren, 104 years old, celebrates with friends on the courthouse steps after registering to vote for the first time in his life.

Bob Fitch, Batesville, Mississippi, 1966

BELOW When the Voting Rights Act of 1965 became the law of the land, federal registrars fanned out across the South. Here Mrs. Jane Jackson of Canton, with her grandson by her side, takes the voter registration oath before a federal registrar. As she left the office, Mrs. Jackson said, "Got to do something. They cut off my pension."

Matt Herron, Canton, Mississippi, 1965

SNCC field secretary Ralph Featherstone, in a
bib overall, and a local supporter carry out a sign
announcing the next day's vote at the Lowndes County
Freedom Organization (LCFO) headquarters. In
overwhelmingly black Lowndes County, LCFO adopted
the black panther symbol to visually represent the
community's goal of acquiring political power.

Bob Fletcher, Lowndes County, Alabama, 1966

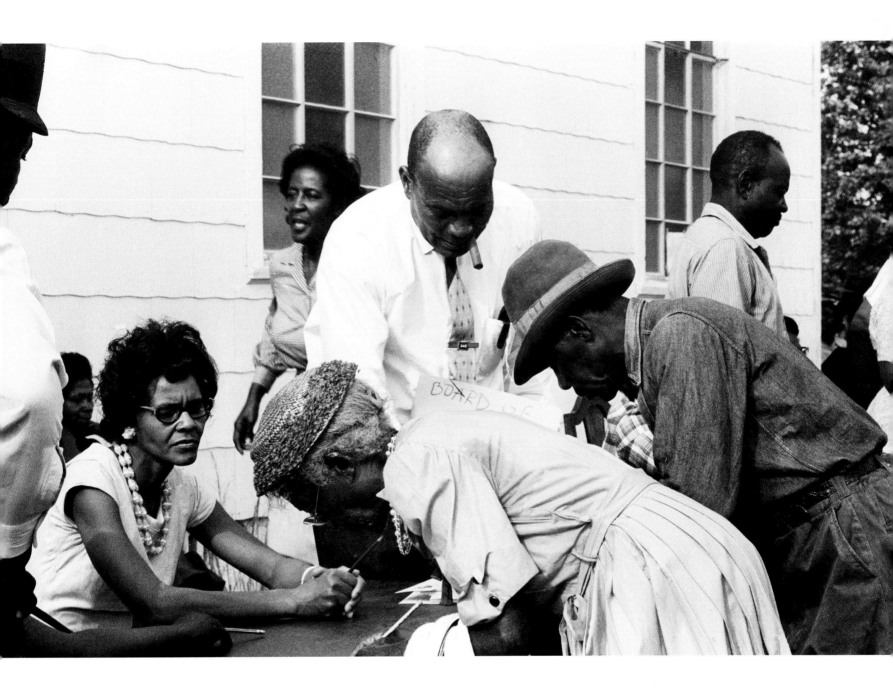

Lowndes County Freedom Organization (LCFO) was
a legal third party formed to challenge the segregated
Alabama Democratic Party. The logo of the Alabama
Democratic Party was a white rooster topped with
the proclamation "White Supremacy for the Right."
LCFO's logo was the original black panther, predating
the Bay Area Black Panther Party. Here party members
fill out primary ballots.

Maria Varela, Lowndes County, Alabama, 1966

ABOVE A woman marks a black panther ballot in the general election. SNCC's Lowndes County Freedom Organization's leaders told voters to simply "vote for the panther."

Maria Varela, Lowndes County, Alabama, 1966

RIGHT For Lowndes County blacks voting for the first time in the twentieth century, the black panther symbolized and encouraged political participation.

Bob Fletcher, Lowndes County, Alabama, 1966

This handbill lists the Holmes County Freedom Democratic Party's slate for the 1967 election. Though unsuccessful in the contest for sheriff, the community did elect the first black representative to the Mississippi legislature since Reconstruction.

Maria Varela, Holmes County, 1967

Part Three:
State and Local Terror

Violence against the freedom movement was systemic. In county after county, so-called forces of law and order turned a blind eye to what can only be called terrorism. The Ku Klux Klan and other white supremacist groups engaged in relentless warfare against change while police departments, sheriffs' departments, and state police authorities frequently worked hand-in-hand with the Klan. In Amite County, where the sheriff's brother headed the Ku Klux Klan, one of SNCC's earliest Mississippi supporters, NAACP leader Herbert Lee, a fifty-two-year-old father of nine children, was shot and killed in broad daylight by a member of the state legislature who was never charged or brought to court. An eyewitness willing to testify against the legislator was later ambushed and killed. "Citizens' Councils" of businessmen, lawmakers, and other "responsible" whites were actually the white-collar face of the Klan. Mississippi and several other states created or revived criminal anarchy and criminal "syndicalism" laws aimed at crushing dissent by making opposition to the government illegal. As one small-town mayor in Mississippi responded to an assertion of constitutional rights: "That law ain't got here yet." That the number of dead was not higher was partly due to one of the little-discussed dimensions of the southern freedom struggle—armed self-defense.

LEFT Ben Chaney, the younger brother of James Earl Chaney, is comforted by his mother during the funeral service.

George Ballis, Meridian, Mississippi, 1964

RIGHT Speaking at the funeral of James Earl Chaney, CORE leader Dave Dennis said, "I have attended these funerals and memorials, and I am sick and tired. . . . The trouble is you are not sick and tired."

George Ballis, Meridian, Mississippi, 1964

LEFT In the burned ruins of Mt. Zion United Methodist Church in Neshoba County, Fannie Lou Chaney speaks at a memorial service for her son James Earl Chaney and co–civil rights workers Michael "Mickey" Schwerner and Andrew Goodman. The three young men were arrested while investigating a fire that burned this church to the ground and, later that same day, they were murdered by a Ku Klux Klan mob.

David Prince, Neshoba County, Mississippi, 1964

BELOW A mourner grieves at the same memorial service for civil rights workers Michael "Mickey" Schwerner, James Earl Chaney, and Andrew Goodman.

David Prince, Neshoba County, Mississippi, 1964

BELOW Neshoba County deputy sheriff Cecil Price watches the memorial service for James Earl Chaney. Himself a Klan member, Price was convicted in 1967 of conspiracy in the three murders and imprisoned.

David Prince, Neshoba County, Mississippi, 1964

RIGHT SNCC leader and COFO project director Bob Moses stands solemnly in the ashes of Mt. Zion before speaking at the memorial service.

Tamio Wakayama, Neshoba County, Mississippi, 1964

In Birmingham the use of fire hoses and dogs
backfired. National outrage caused President John
Kennedy to denounce segregation—the first U.S.
president to do so—and to urge its legal ban.

**Bob Adelman, Kelly Ingram Park, Birmingham, Alabama,
1963**

Despite force and violence by police and firemen,
protestors hold onto each other and withstand the full
fury of the water.

**Bob Adelman, Kelly Ingram Park, Birmingham, Alabama,
1963**

ABOVE White hecklers insult two young women who are part of a voting rights drive.

Bob Adelman, Selma, Alabama, 1965

RIGHT A picketer is arrested behind Loveman's Department Store. Civil rights leaders believed that if they could break segregation in Birmingham, it would collapse throughout the South.

Bob Adelman, Birmingham, Alabama, 1963

A young woman penned in by Sheriff Jim Clark's posse glares as her fellow demonstrators chant, "No more Jim Clark over me." Clark was eventually convicted of drug smuggling.

Bob Adelman, Selma, Alabama, 1965

In January 1966 nearly one hundred homeless former plantation workers occupied the decommissioned Greenville, Mississippi, air force base, demanding the base be made available for homeless families. They also asked for land, job training, and jobs. They were evicted at the request of the U.S. Justice Department.

Maria Varela, Washington County, Mississippi, 1966

The U.S. military evicted more than one hundred
plantation workers from the Greenville air force base.
"People are hungry in the Delta," a protestor told the
Justice Department representative.

Maria Varela, Washington County, Mississippi, 1966

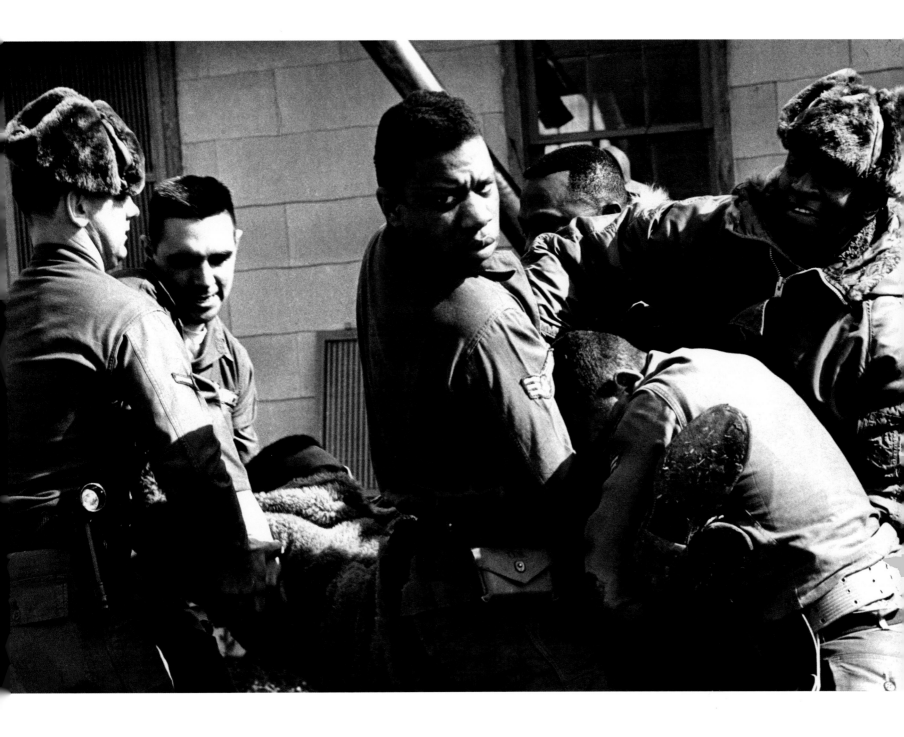

Military police carry off a protestor from the barracks occupied by evicted farm laborers and civil rights workers.

Maria Varela, Washington County, Mississippi, 1966

LEFT Troopers from the Louisiana Highway Patrol wait to escort civil rights marchers through Bogalusa, Louisiana. Later in the march, the tall trooper in the center used his club on the photographer.

Matt Herron, Bogalusa, Louisiana, 1965

RIGHT March participants sing during a Deacons for Defense march through Bogalusa. Song was the glue that helped hold the civil rights community together. It fostered courage in times of danger, solidarity in times of stress.

Matt Herron, Bogalusa, Louisiana, 1965

BELOW Louisiana Highway Patrol officer with automatic weapon "guards" marchers as they pass through Bogalusa.

Matt Herron, Bogalusa, Louisiana, 1965

RIGHT A segregationist and her daughters watch marchers in Bogalusa. Her sign reads: "Nigger Don't You Wish You Were White." She wanted to get her message out, and the photographer was happy to comply.

Matt Herron, Bogalusa, Louisiana, 1965

LEFT Protesting denial of the right to vote, Aylene Quinn of McComb, Mississippi, and her children sit on the steps of Mississippi governor Paul Johnson's mansion. Five-year-old Anthony Quinn sits beside Dr. June Finer of the Medical Committee for Human Rights.

Matt Herron, Jackson, Mississippi, 1965

RIGHT

1. Patrolman Huey Krohn tries to take a small American flag held by Anthony Quinn. Out of sight, his mother is saying, "Anthony, don't let that man take your flag."

2. When Anthony refuses to give up his flag, the patrolman goes berserk, wrenching it out of his hands. This picture was a winner in the 1965 World Press Photo Contest.

3. Dr. Finer comforts Anthony. She had joined the Quinns' protest in order to be arrested. Denied access to the fairgrounds where demonstrators were being held, Finer used her own arrest to treat demonstrators who were being denied medical treatment.

Matt Herron, Jackson, Mississippi, 1965

ABOVE Jackson police drag demonstrators to the "nigger wagon." One hundred and fifteen people were arrested as protesters tried to fill the jails in an attempt to bring an end to segregation in Jackson.

Matt Herron, Jackson, Mississippi, 1965

RIGHT Going "limp," demonstrators nonviolently resist arrest and force police to drag them to the "nigger wagon." Here a policeman appears as if he is about to stomp on a young woman.

Matt Herron, Jackson, Mississippi, 1965

Police surround demonstrators in the "nigger wagon."
For the demonstrators jail signals a victory, not a
defeat.

Matt Herron, Jackson, Mississippi, 1965

Coretta Scott King sits with Rosa Parks shortly after her husband, Rev. Martin Luther King, was assassinated in Memphis. The women were flying to Atlanta in a private jet loaned them by the Kennedy family.

Bob Fitch, Between Memphis, Tennessee, and Atlanta, Georgia, 1968

ABOVE Coretta Scott King sits with Rosa Parks.

Bob Fitch, Between Memphis, Tennessee, and Atlanta, Georgia, 1968

RIGHT Family members and supporters gather in Coretta King's bedroom before the funeral. (Left to right) King's son, Martin III; King's brother, Alfred Daniel King; Coretta Scott King; Rev. Ralph Abernathy; and SCLC staff members. On the table is the *New York Times* account of Rev. Martin Luther King's assassination.

Bob Fitch, Atlanta, Georgia, 1968

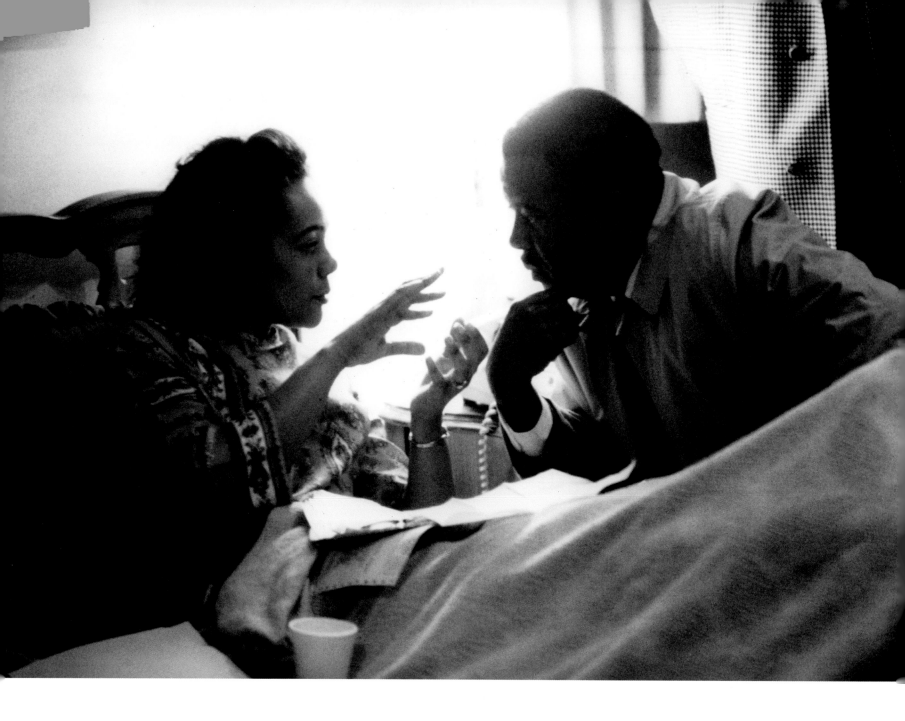

ABOVE Coretta Scott King consults in her bedroom with Rev. Ralph Abernathy about Atlanta funeral arrangements.

Bob Fitch, Atlanta, Georgia, 1968

RIGHT Coretta Scott King rests in her bed prior to the funeral. On the wall, there is a portrait of her as a younger woman.

Bob Fitch, Atlanta, Georgia, 1968

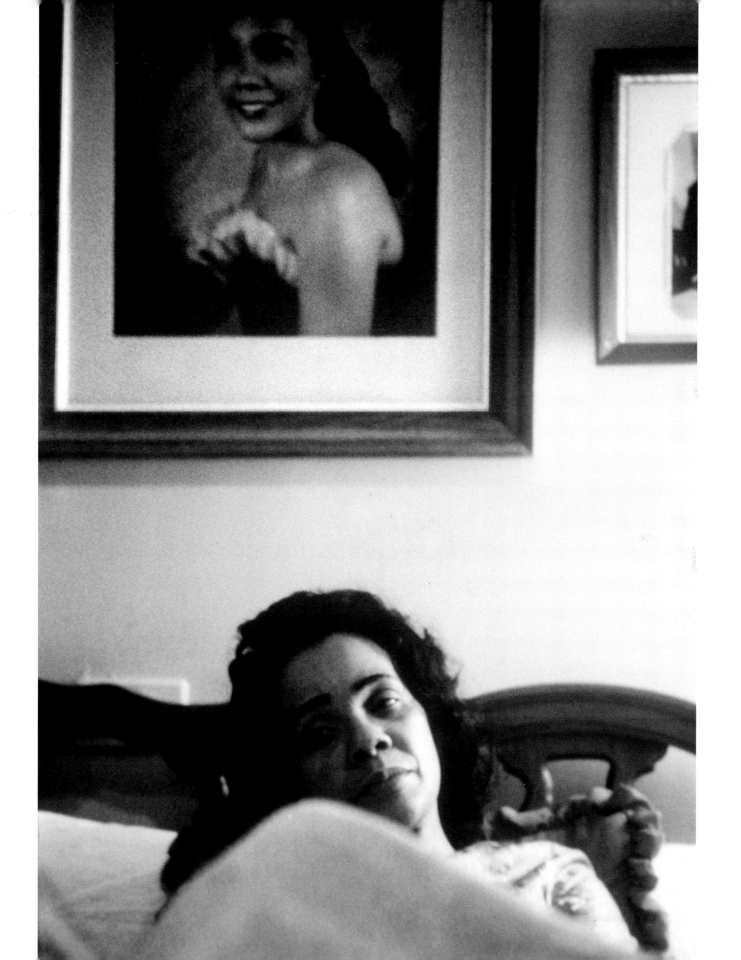

Rev. Martin Luther King, Sr., stands with his wife,
Alberta Williams King, at their son's funeral in
Atlanta, Georgia.

Bob Fitch, Atlanta, Georgia, 1968

Leaving church after the funeral service are (left to right): Coretta Scott King; Alberta Williams King, King's mother; and Christine Farras, King's sister.

Bob Fitch, Atlanta, Georgia, 1968

ABOVE At the funeral service are (left to right): Rev. Martin Luther King's daughters, Bernice and Yolanda, son, Martin III, and Coretta Scott King.

Bob Fitch, Atlanta, Georgia, 1968

RIGHT During the funeral service, Coretta Scott King comforts her daughter Bernice.

Bob Fitch, Atlanta, Georgia, 1968

"The king of love is dead," sang Nina Simone, and the murder of Rev. Martin Luther King on April 4, 1968, in Memphis, Tennessee, almost certainly ended an era. However, behind the dismay and tears and anger, an enduring political strength and commitment to justice remained. The day before her husband's funeral in Atlanta, Georgia, Coretta Scott King returned to Memphis to march with striking sanitation workers whose cause her husband had supported.

Bob Fitch, Atlanta, Georgia, 1968

Part Four: **Meredith March against Fear and Black Power**

On June 5, 1966, James Meredith, who in 1962 became the first black student to enroll at the University of Mississippi, set out from Memphis, Tennessee, for Jackson, Mississippi, on a solitary "March against Fear." Meredith sought to show that in the new era blacks in America could walk, and register to vote, without fear of intimidation and reprisal. He walked twelve miles on his first day and reached the Tennessee-Mississippi border. The following day, sixteen miles inside the state of Mississippi, he was ambushed and wounded with birdshot. Martin Luther King, Floyd McKissick, CORE's new national director, and Stokely Carmichael, SNCC's newly elected chairman, decided to continue Meredith's march. This was more complex than a protest. Passage of the 1964 Civil Rights Act and the 1965 Voting Rights Act was changing the South's political climate. "Victory," however, had created uncertainty. All during the march there was discussion, debate, and a question: "Where do we go from here?" The two civil rights bills, while necessary reform, were clearly insufficient to solve the problems of poverty and lack of economic opportunity so easily seen all along the march route. Nor had antiblack violence diminished by much. The year had begun with NAACP leader Vernon Dahmer's murder in Hattiesburg when Klansmen firebombed his home. However, old habits of fear and deference were eroding. The national Democratic Party had said it would no longer tolerate racism and its "Dixiecrats" had fled to the Republican Party. Meanwhile, within the black community "black consciousness" was strengthening. One significant sign of changing attitudes was the presence of the Deacons for Defense and Justice on the march. Formed by black World War II veterans in 1964 in Jonesboro, Louisiana, to protect that community and members of CORE from Ku Klux Klan violence, these men had come—with the approval of march leaders—to protect and defend Meredith marchers.

Following his shooting, James Meredith returned to continue his "March against Fear."

Bob Fitch, Near Canton, Mississippi, 1966

LEFT In Canton, surrounded by press and supporters during a break in the Meredith March, Rev. Martin Luther King greets Annie Devine, who emerged from Canton and became one of the Mississippi movement's most powerful leaders.

Bob Fitch, Near Canton, Mississippi, 1966

BELOW Meredith marchers exuberantly enter Jackson, the capital of Mississippi. (Left to right) Mrs. Abernathy; Rev. Ralph Abernathy; Coretta Scott King; Rev. Martin Luther King, president of SCLC; Floyd McKissick, chairman of CORE; and Stokely Carmichael, chairman of SNCC.

Bob Fitch, Jackson, Mississippi, 1966

Elbow to elbow stand Walter Reuther, president of the
United Auto Workers, Rev. Ralph Abernathy, and Rev.
Martin Luther King.

Bob Fitch, Near Jackson, Mississippi, 1966

March leaders share a joke. (Left to right) Hosea Williams, Bernard Lee (personal aide to King), Rev. Martin Luther King, Stokely Carmichael, and Willie Ricks.

Bob Fitch, Near Canton, Mississippi, 1966

In a private home near Canton, Mississippi, march leaders discuss and debate national and local reaction to Stokely Carmichael's call for "Black Power." Clockwise from left are: Bernard Lee, Andrew Young, Robert Green, Rev. Martin Luther King, Lawrence Guyot, and Stokely Carmichael (lying on floor).

Bob Fitch, Near Canton, Mississippi, 1966

Marchers sing freedom songs en route to Jackson.

Matt Herron, Near Jackson, Mississippi, 1966

LEFT Photographer Maria Varela noticed a new demographic on the Meredith March: "In previous marches, you didn't get the eighteen-to-twenty-five-year-olds. They weren't nonviolent, and they didn't feel like they could go on the marches. So you'd have a lot of women, children, teenagers, and some older men. But once the idea of Black Power appeared, we saw them coming out of the woodwork."

Bob Fitch, Near Canton, Mississippi, 1966

ABOVE Fear seems to have been erased as marchers are about to enter Jackson, the final leg of the march.

Matt Herron, Near Jackson, Mississippi, 1966

Marching children frame state police sharpshooter.

Maria Varela, Near Jackson, Mississippi, 1966

After two hundred miles of Mississippi highway, Meredith marchers enter outskirts of Jackson.

Bob Fitch, Near Jackson, Mississippi, 1966

LEFT "Ain't gonna let no rain turn us around."

Maria Varela, Near Canton, Mississippi, 1966

ABOVE Marchers struggle through a rainstorm between Canton and Tougaloo, Mississippi.

Maria Varela, Near Canton, Mississippi, 1966

LEFT After hours of rain, the emerging sun reflects marchers in a puddle.

Maria Varela, Near Canton, Mississippi, 1966

BELOW Defying local authorities and the threat of police violence, marchers begin to erect a tent for overnight stay at the McNeal Elementary School in Canton. At center are (left to right): Stokely Carmichael, Floyd McKissick, and Rev. Martin Luther King.

Matt Herron, Canton, Mississippi, 1966

LEFT Victims react to a tear gas attack by the Mississippi Highway Patrol. Troopers used CNS gas, the same toxic gas used by U.S. troops against the Vietcong in Vietnam.

Matt Herron, Canton, Mississippi, 1966

BELOW Troopers of the Mississippi Highway Patrol prepare for a tear gas attack on Meredith marchers, who, though denied permission to use McNeal Elementary School for their overnight camp, began erecting tents anyway.

Matt Herron, Canton, Mississippi, 1966

LEFT At march's end, Stokley Carmichael delivers a Black Power speech in front of the state capitol building.

Matt Herron, Jackson, Mississippi, 1966

BELOW At a night rally in Greenwood, SNCC chairman Stokely Carmichael first uses the phrase "Black Power" in a public speech. "It was nothing new," Carmichael later explained. "We'd been talking about nothing else in the Delta for years. The only difference was that this time the national media was there."

Bob Fitch, Greenwood, Mississippi, 1966

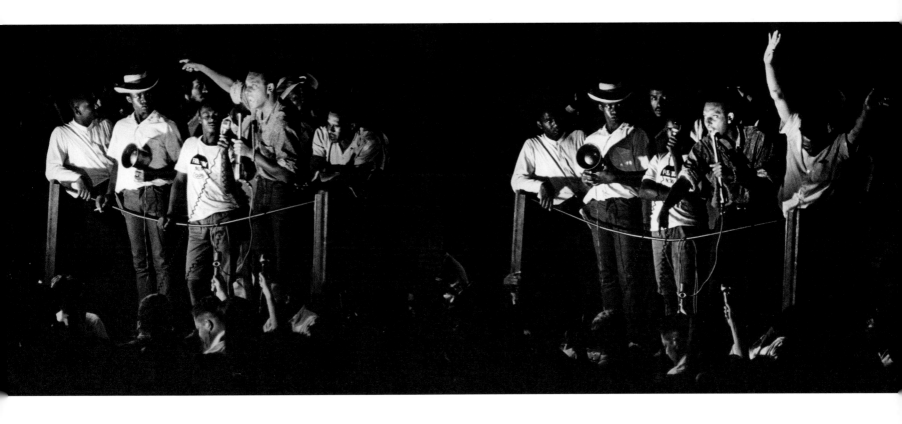

LEFT Sneaking out from her home to attend SNCC meetings when she was fourteen years old, June Johnson of Greenwood, Mississippi, now seventeen, personified the young, indigenous leadership which fueled Mississippi's Civil Rights Movement.

Maria Varela, Near Canton, Mississippi, 1966

ABOVE White supremacists give the finger to marchers at a final rally before the Mississippi state capitol in Jackson.

Matt Herron, Jackson, Mississippi, 1966

BELOW Onlookers and white supremacists harass a news photographer while Mississippi Highway Patrolmen, in the background, guard the capitol.

Matt Herron, Jackson, Mississippi, 1966

RIGHT A hand-drawn black panther indicates a change of movement symbolism as young men joined the Meredith March in response to the call for Black Power.

Maria Varela, Near Canton, Mississippi, 1966

Like the civil rights revolution itself, the marches owed their success to the participation of thousands of ordinary people. Here, marchers line the horizon en route from Selma to Montgomery, Alabama.

Matt Herron, Alabama, 1965

SNCC's enduring impact is best understood as the legacy of grassroots organizing. Within this frame, SNCC and the field organizers of CORE, SCLC, and the NAACP are really an interconnected force that in just one intense decade *successfully* challenged and changed America for the better.

Putting their lives at risk, this relatively small group broke the back of a racist system that was tolerated at the highest levels of government.

Indeed, the MFDP and that party's 1964 challenge led to a two-party system in the South and forced changes in political rules and practices that have permanently expanded the participation of women and minorities.

Other social justice movements gained strength from the pool of ideas found in the movement. Chicano farm workers, who were facing sheriffs and going to jail in the late 1950s, invited SNCC workers to help with their efforts in the late 1960s. Discussion of sexism and women's rights within SNCC and SNCC's real-life examples of empowered, respected women, encouraged a burgeoning feminist movement.

Student struggle, also inspired by the southern movement, expanded and accelerated. Students for a Democratic Society's (SDS) grassroots Educational and Research Action Projects (ERAP) in the North grew out of discussions with SNCC and observation of its work. The Northern Student Movement formed in 1961 to aid SNCC became an activist organization with nearly fifty campus chapters taking on welfare reform and dysfunctional schools. The Free Speech Movement that erupted on the University of California campus at Berkeley during the 1964–65 school year was initiated by a Mississippi Freedom Summer volunteer.

SNCC's articulation of "Black Power" fostered a militant black consciousness that strengthened possibilities of activism among Native Americans and Chicanos. The Black Studies and Ethnic Studies departments on college campuses today have roots in the freedom schools, citizenship schools, and the general idea of education for liberation.

And more than anything else the movement's legacy is found in its veterans. Once young and mentored by "elders" who had labored in the fields of social change, these 1960s veterans are now elders themselves who are passing on the precious legacy summarized by Ella Baker's words: "We who believe in freedom cannot rest until it comes."

Reflection: **How I First Saw King and Found the Movement**

Clayborne Carson

The photographs in *This Light of Ours* evoke memories of a Southern Freedom Movement that enabled ordinary people—some of them landless peasants—to become extraordinary participants in the American democratic experiment. Although the subjects featured in this splendid collection include national leaders such as Martin Luther King, Jr., the images also draw attention to the grassroots leaders, community organizers, white volunteers from northern colleges, and many others of all ages who made crucial contributions to a historic movement. Talented photographers (many of them white), often collaborating with their subjects (mostly black), created images that revealed the movement's complexities while at the same time exposing the fundamental contradiction between America's egalitarian founding ideals and its shameful racial realities. *This Light of Ours* shows the movement coming together during the early and mid-1960s and offers hints of the internal conflicts that tore it apart by the end of the decade.

Although I grew up as one of the few black residents of a small town in New Mexico, some of the photographs in this collection stimulated thoughts about my own family's transgenerational journey from the South to find better opportunities elsewhere. My parents wanted to shield their children from the Jim Crow system they had left behind. As a child, Dad had moved from Tuscaloosa, Alabama, when his father migrated to Detroit to take a job at the Ford Motor Company. After being drafted during World War II, Dad left

Detroit and took advantage of an unexpected opportunity to enter a newly established black officer training program. While assigned to a base in Alabama, he met Mom, who had moved from rural Florida in search of wartime job opportunities. Soon after the war, he accepted a job in New Mexico as a security inspector at the Los Alamos Scientific Laboratory, which was then shifting from military to civilian control. Raising their children in a pleasant, overwhelmingly white, government-owned approximation of the American suburban ideal, my parents rarely mentioned the news reports of racial conflicts that were occurring elsewhere during the 1950s.

Although I was a precocious child who perused the newspapers I delivered, my parents could hardly have expected that I would be fascinated and inspired by news reports about the Little Rock Nine who desegregated Central High School in 1957, the four Greensboro teenagers who ignited the sit-in protests in 1960, and the Freedom Riders who captured the nation's attention during the spring and summer of 1961. I was also thrilled to see King's portrait on the cover of *Time* magazine in the aftermath of the Montgomery bus boycott or to watch him being interviewed on *Meet the Press* and other television programs. I was proud that King and the protesting students were among the few African Americans deemed worthy of having their pictures in the local newspapers or in the *Life* and *Ebony* magazines that came to our home. I imagined that I might someday also play some prominent role in the Civil Rights Movement or perhaps attract attention as "the first Negro" to do what only white people had done.

Enrolling in the fall of 1962 at the University of New Mexico, I became involved in student politics and joined the small campus community of civil rights proponents. I learned about SNCC and even met one of the founders of Students for a Democratic Society, but nonetheless felt relegated to the sidelines while southern black students were spearheading sustained protests. It was impossible to ignore the news photographs of the Birmingham teenagers who braved police dogs and fire hoses during the spring of 1963. When I learned that the widespread civil rights demonstrations taking place throughout the nation would culminate at the end of August in a massive March on Washington, I also realized that I would be a delegate at the National Student Association annual meeting to be held in Indiana just a few days before the march and less than a thousand miles away. Although I sur-

MARCH ON WASHINGTON FOR JOBS AND FREEDOM
AUGUST 28, 1963
LINCOLN MEMORIAL PROGRAM

1.	The National Anthem	*Led by* Marian Anderson.
2.	Invocation	The Very Rev. Patrick O'Boyle, *Archbishop of Washington.*
3.	Opening Remarks	A. Philip Randolph, *Director March on Washington for Jobs and Freedom.*
4.	Remarks	Dr. Eugene Carson Blake, *Stated Clerk, United Presbyterian Church of the U.S.A.; Vice Chairman, Commission on Race Relations of the National Council of Churches of Christ in America.*
5.	Tribute to Negro Women Fighters for Freedom Daisy Bates Diane Nash Bevel Mrs. Medgar Evers Mrs. Herbert Lee Rosa Parks Gloria Richardson	Mrs. Medgar Evers
6.	Remarks	John Lewis, *National Chairman, Student Nonviolent Coordinating Committee.*
7.	Remarks	Walter Reuther, *President, United Automobile, Aerospace and Agricultural Implement Wokers of America, AFL-CIO; Chairman, Industrial Union Department, AFL-CIO.*
8.	Remarks	James Farmer, *National Director, Congress of Racial Equality.*
9.	Selection	Eva Jessye *Choir*
10.	Prayer	Rabbi Uri Miller, *President Synagogue Council of America.*
11.	Remarks	Whitney M. Young, Jr., *Executive Director, National Urban League.*
12.	Remarks	Mathew Ahmann, *Executive Director, National Catholic Conference for Interracial Justice.*
13.	Remarks	Roy Wilkins, *Executive Secretary, National Association for the Advancement of Colored People.*
14.	Selection	Miss Mahalia Jackson
15.	Remarks	Rabbi Joachim Prinz, *President American Jewish Congress.*
16.	Remarks	The Rev. Dr. Martin Luther King, Jr., *President, Southern Christian Leadership Conference.*
17.	The Pledge	A Philip Randolph
18.	Benediction	Dr. Benjamin E. Mays, *President, Morehouse College.*

"WE SHALL OVERCOME"

mised that my participation in a racial demonstration would worry my parents, especially my sometimes overbearing mother, I could not let the opportunity pass. I didn't tell either of them about my plan to join an NAACP group from Indianapolis on an overnight chartered bus to the Washington Mall.

I would later take pride in having been present on August 28, 1963, when King delivered his "I Have a Dream" speech, but my attention had already been drawn to other, less prominent participants in the March on Washington. Although the event became best known as the occasion for King's oration, it also introduced me to an African American freedom struggle that King did not initiate or control. King's remarkable achievements eventually became the focus of my scholarly life, and his visionary ideas would profoundly influence my worldview, but I initially saw the freedom struggle from the perspective of grassroots organizers affiliated with SNCC, the underfunded but dynamic competitor to King's Southern Christian Leadership Conference (SCLC). My life became entwined with SNCC as its staff members became models for my own activism, subjects for my scholarly research, and, in some instances, friends for life.

A few days before the march, while attending the National Student Association's annual convention at the University of Indiana, I met several SNCC activists, and was particularly impressed by Stokely Carmichael, the articulate, self-confident Howard University philosophy major who exemplified SNCC's brash militancy. When I told him that I wanted to attend the march, Stokely deprecated it as a "middle-class picnic" and urged me instead to volunteer for SNCC's organizing efforts in places such as Albany (Georgia), Cambridge (Maryland), Danville (Virginia), and Greenwood (Mississippi). I found it difficult to admit that participating in the "picnic" would be the most adventurous thing I'd ever done. Although I was not yet ready to join SNCC's "field secretaries" on the frontlines of campaigns against southern white racial supremacy, Stokely's remarks changed my view of the march and all that followed it.

As I marched in the steamy heat amidst thousands of strangers, I felt alone yet also intensely curious about every aspect of the unprecedented gathering of civil rights advocates. Most of all, I was impressed by the enormous variety of marchers—people of all ages, white as well as black—most of them well-dressed (as for church rather than a picnic). I was amazed to see far more black faces in one day than I had seen during my entire childhood.

Because of my previous contacts with Stokely and other SNCC activists, I paid special attention to a contingent of Mississippi voting rights proponents whose contagious revelry energized the marchers and lightened the overall mood of somber seriousness and high-minded solemnity. While most marchers slowly repeated the verses of "We Shall Overcome" as we strolled toward the Lincoln Memorial, the Mississippians snaked through the crowd singing more animated freedom songs: "*I woke up this morning with my mind stayed on freedom*" or "*I've got the light of freedom; I'm gonna let it shine!*" Although I had previously thought that black Mississippians lived in oppressive conditions only slightly removed from slavery, they displayed an appealing eagerness to let their light of freedom shine.

Pushing forward as close as I could get to the speakers' platform, I was able to see glimpses of famous Hollywood stars—such as Charlton Heston, Harry Belafonte, and Sidney Poitier—and listen to the long program of remarks by black leaders I had read or heard about. I was also excited to hear well-known singers—Mahalia Jackson, Joan Baez, Bob Dylan, Peter, Paul, and Mary—some of whom I had watched on the *Ed Sullivan Show*. I recognized a few of the names of the "Negro Women Fighters for Freedom" who were introduced to the crowd by the event's only female speaker, Josephine Baker (I would only later learn of her achievements).

Even with my limited understanding of African American history, I sensed the unique significance of the remarkable assemblage of great black leaders on the platform. Nonetheless, I felt a special anticipation when the venerable labor leader A. Philip Randolph introduced twenty-three-year-old John Lewis, SNCC's newly elected chair. John was, by a decade, the youngest speaker on the long program. I felt proud of him as he forcefully expressed SNCC's identification with grassroots struggles that were receiving scant attention in the national media. He cautioned marchers that "we have nothing to be proud of for hundreds and thousands of our brothers are not here. They have no money for their transportation, for they are receiving starvation wages, or no wages at all."

Older black leaders generally saw the march as an effort to support the Kennedy administration's proposed civil rights legislation, but John emphasized the bill's limitations: "The voting section of this bill will not help thousands of black citizens who want to vote. It will not help the citizens of Mississippi, of Alabama and Georgia, who are qualified to vote but lack a sixth-grade education. 'ONE MAN, ONE VOTE' is the African cry. It is ours, too."

He condemned conventional "politicians who build their careers on immoral compromises and ally themselves with open forms of political, economic, and social exploitation." He complained that the Democratic Party of Kennedy was also the party of Mississippi segregationist Senator James Eastland, while the Republican Party of New York liberal Jacob Javits was also the party of staunchly conservative Arizona Senator Barry Goldwater. "Where is our party?" he bluntly asked. "We cannot depend on any political party, for both the Democrats and the Republicans have betrayed the basic principles of the Declaration of Independence."

Years later, John would explain to me that his original draft had been even stronger in its criticisms of the Kennedy administration but was softened at the insistence of march leaders. He was persuaded to delete his warnings that "the revolution is at hand" and that the Southern Freedom Movement would "not wait for the President, the Justice Department, nor Congress, but we will take matters into our hands and create a source of power, outside of any national structure, that could and would assure us of victory."

Even in its softened form, John's speech was still a powerful statement of SNCC's distinctive militancy. For John, as for other SNCC workers, real progress required grassroots activism rather than reform legislation achieved through top-down decision making. "We all recognize the fact that if any radical social, political and economic changes are to take place in our society, the people, the masses, must bring them about," he explained. "In the struggle, we must seek more than civil rights; we must work for the community of love, peace and true brotherhood. Our minds, souls and hearts cannot rest until freedom and justice exist for *all people.*"

Introduced to Gandhian and Christian precepts by James Lawson, the black divinity student who conducted nonviolence workshops in Nashville during the late 1950s, John had a principled commitment to nonviolent principles that would prove unshakable. He had been arrested during the sit-ins, brutally beaten during the initial Freedom Ride, and then imprisoned in Mississippi along with hundreds of other Freedom Riders who came to the state during the summer of 1961. John concluded his speech by stressing the revolutionary possibilities of nonviolent resistance on a massive scale:

We will not stop. If we do not get meaningful legislation out of this Congress, the time will come when we will not confine our marching to Washington. We will march through the South, through the streets of Jackson, through the streets of Danville, through the streets of Cambridge, through the streets of Birmingham. But we will march with the spirit of love and with the spirit of dignity that we have shown here today.

By the force of our demands, our determination and our numbers, we shall splinter the desegregated South into a thousand pieces and put them back together in the image of God and democracy.

We must say, "Wake up, America. Wake up! For we cannot stop, and we will not be patient."

After John's rousing speech, I still looked forward to King's concluding remarks but, to my continuing regret, couldn't give his oration the attention it deserved. Exhausted at the end of a long, hot afternoon, I worried that I would not be able to find the bus that had brought me. I remember walking away from the Lincoln Memorial as Randolph introduced King as "the moral leader of our nation." As I listened to the loud cheers that greeted King and heard the familiar sound of his voice, I tried my best to avoid being left behind in an unfamiliar city. After King had finished and the program concluded, I met a stranger who sensed my desperation and said that there was a seat available on his bus. I was only a bit concerned that this bus was headed not to Indianapolis but to Penn Station in New York.

The march unexpectedly became the start of an

extended adventure that involved staying overnight in Harlem, exchanging my original bus ticket for a ticket back to Indiana, and then hitchhiking more than a thousand miles to Albuquerque's downtown bus station, where I called my parents to tell them that I had just returned.

Only later did I comprehend the full significance of King's mostly extemporaneous remarks, but even then other aspects of the march shaped my memories of it. Drawn immediately to SNCC's militancy and its distinctive style of grassroots organizing, I would only gradually develop an understanding of King's enduring legacy. The march was the abrupt start of an adulthood that would have been unimaginable in 1963—when there were no black professors and no courses in African American history at UCLA or at Stanford, where I would later teach. My search for the deeper meanings of the March on Washington would eventually lead me to new insights about SNCC, King, and the long history of African American freedom struggles.

After returning to New Mexico, I began to see myself as an activist and continued to seek information about SNCC's work in the South. Late in the fall of 1963, I traveled to a meeting in New Orleans that focused on bringing hundreds of students to Mississippi during the following summer for a major voting rights effort. The trip gave me a brief opportunity to protest southern segregation by joining a picket line outside a theater. At the meeting, I listened for the first time to Bob Moses, the SNCC organizer who had left a high school teaching job in New York to become a key figure in the Mississippi voting rights movement. Although Stokely had impressed me with his brash assertiveness, Bob's soft-spoken commitment to bottom-up organizing had a more enduring impact on my evolving worldview. His desire to downplay his own central role sharply contrasted with SCLC's reliance on King's charismatic leadership.

Bob drew attention to the veteran NAACP leaders in Mississippi—Amzie Moore of Cleveland, Aaron Henry of Clarksdale, and others—who had invited him and his SNCC colleagues to assist their ongoing voter registration efforts. After arriving in McComb

during the summer of 1961, he had recruited a cadre of dedicated young organizers, including Charles McLaurin, Hollis Watkins, John Hardy, Curtis Hayes, Charles Cobb, Sam Block, and Willie Peacock. During 1962 SNCC joined with other civil rights groups to form the Council of Federated Organizations (COFO) to coordinate Mississippi voting rights activities. Bob became the director of COFO's field staff.

Hearing Moses describe plans for the summer project, I quickly sensed the special respect he had earned from other activists. This high regard resulted not only from his willingness to take great risks on behalf of the movement but also from his genuine concern for the Mississippians who worked with him. Faced with deadly segregationist terrorism, he knew that the Mississippi movement needed outside help but was also concerned that poor, ill-educated black residents would become dependent on the college-educated voting rights workers already arriving from outside the state. The New Orleans gathering reinforced the lesson I had learned from the Washington march—that King's national prominence obscured the important roles of resilient local movements spurred by self-reliant grassroots leaders who did not look to King and other national civil rights leaders for guidance. Bob's remarkable ability to nurture the development of local leaders would influence a generation of community organizers in the North as well as the South.

Although I considered volunteering for the 1964 Mississippi Summer Project, I also worried that full-time activism would distract me from becoming the first member of my family to graduate from college. Nonetheless, my infatuation with SNCC's distinctive qualities and its adventurous spirit grew ever stronger. Like other members of "Friends of SNCC" groups, my ties to the group were strengthened by the sympathetic reporters and photographers who publicized SNCC's projects. (Given how much SNCC accomplished with so few material resources, I wonder sometimes what it could have done with modern Internet communications technology.)

SNCC may have lacked the national media coverage given to King, but, as can be seen by the splendid photographs in this collection, it was fortunate to attract an exceptionally talented group of artists and writers to its cause. The powerful images on SNCC's posters— ONE MAN ONE VOTE; COME LET US BUILD A NEW WORLD TOGETHER—decorated my walls for many years to come, and SNCC's NOW poster would later provide the image for the cover of my book on SNCC.

Reading articles in SNCC's newspaper, *The Student Voice*, and in its other publications, I and many others gained an understanding of the southern freedom struggle that corrected simplistic King-centered perspectives. I learned that SNCC's organizing efforts spawned sustained movements in communities where King never came and where movements would continue long after the passage of national civil rights legislation.

My summer adventure increased my eagerness to leave the racial isolation I felt in New Mexico. Returning to college for my sophomore year, I became increasingly involved in campus politics while considering options for the future. After a failed attempt during the fall of 1964 to join the Peace Corps, I accepted my older sister's invitation to visit her and her family in Los Angeles. After I found a part-time job and transferred to UCLA, my visit lengthened to a permanent stay in California. Living off-campus in West Los Angeles, I sought opportunities to make contact with the freedom struggle I had learned about the previous year. Although civil rights protests were less evident in Southern California than in the San Francisco Bay Area, it did not take long to find a small activist community seeking to shake up the city.

My job at Audience Studies, an advertising research company affiliated with Columbia Pictures, brought me in contact with Charles Samuelson, a member of the Nonviolent Action Committee. N-VAC was founded by three black activists—Woody Coleman, Robert Hall, and Danny Gray—who wanted to break free of the constraints of the predominantly white local affiliate of the Congress of Racial Equality (CORE). Because several N-VAC members had worked with SNCC in the

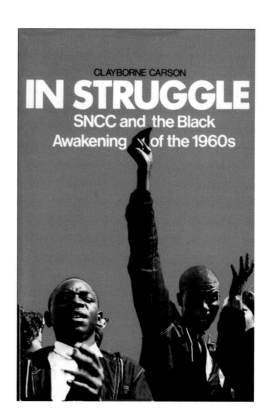

South, N-VAC's approach to organizing was influenced by SNCC's southern projects. N-VAC's membership included whites, such as Charlie, but was limited to those willing to engage in civil disobedience.

N-VAC became my substitute for SNCC, but the sprawling neighborhoods of black Los Angeles offered a quite different organizing challenge than did small southern towns. We focused our efforts on ending employment discrimination rather than fighting southern-style segregation. My initiation ceremony was a sit-in intended to shut down a Thriftymart grocery store in suburban Santa Ana. The small, overwhelmed local police force chose not to arrest us after we had succeeded in discouraging most shoppers from entering for several hours. Although my first arrest would come later, I was accepted into a community of activists and felt closer to my heroes in SNCC.

Although I continued living in West Los Angeles, working in Hollywood, and occasionally attending classes at UCLA, the times I spent at N-VAC's office on

Central Avenue became a special part of my life, exposing me for the first time to urban racial realities. I became acquainted with many of the city's black activists, among them my uncle, Walt Walker, a struggling artist, and his outspoken wife, Jane. Occasional visits to the Aquarius Bookstore on Santa Barbara Avenue also increased my awareness of the burgeoning local black nationalist movement.

The shifting political mood of black Los Angeles reflected the radicalization of SNCC during the period after the March on Washington. After organizing the Mississippi Freedom Democratic Party (MFDP), SNCC workers spearheaded the crucial 1964 Mississippi Summer Project that I had heard about in New Orleans. While the summer volunteers were still in training, three voting rights workers were murdered near Philadelphia, Mississippi. The Summer Project itself was disrupted by hundreds of arrests and more than two dozen bombings of homes and churches in black communities. Nonetheless, COFO organizers were able to bring MFDP delegates to the Democratic Party's convention in Atlantic City. Their goal was to win sufficient support at the convention to unseat the all-white "regular" delegation from Mississippi.

At the August convention, President Lyndon Johnson refused to support the MFDP challenge and instead offered the delegation two at-large seats. MFDP supporters felt betrayed and rejected the compromise. Fannie Lou Hamer, the former sharecropper who joined SNCC's staff after being beaten in retaliation for attempting to register to vote, famously announced, "We didn't come all this way for no two seats." The setback at Atlantic City was a crucial turning point for SNCC and its supporters, because it reinforced their distrust of liberal politicians unwilling to take risks on behalf of the civil rights cause.

Years later, John Lewis would tell me that the lesson of Atlantic City was that "when you play the game and go by the rules, you still can lose, if you don't have the resources, if you're going to disrupt the natural order of things." Stokely saw the setback as more evidence that black Americans could not rely on

"the national conscience" or on "labor, liberal, and civil rights" allies with close ties to the national Democratic Party. As SNCC's relations with mainstream Democrats deteriorated, some in the group began to question nonviolent principles and interracialism.

As SNCC workers deliberated their future, the group's supporters throughout the nation soon heard vivid accounts of the heated debates that took place at SNCC's November staff retreat held in Waveland, Mississippi. Racial and class tensions festered in SNCC as dozens of the white volunteers decided to remain in Mississippi, dramatically changing the racial composition of the staff. Black community organizers questioned the decision-making role of the staff members at SNCC's Atlanta headquarters. In one of the position papers distributed at the meeting, an Alabama activist referred to the "ethnic relationship" between black organizers and the black community and asserted, "I do not feel that this relationship can be entered into by whites." Because of the ties between SNCC and N-VAC, such sentiments soon affected discussions among Los Angeles activists.

The changing mood within the freedom struggle was evident in the Selma-to-Montgomery voting rights march that began late in the spring of 1965. We didn't know then, but that march and the voting rights legislation resulting from it were the last major achievements of the interracial civil rights coalition that had planned the March on Washington. Although both SCLC and SNCC were involved in the Alabama voting rights campaign, relations between the two groups soured as SNCC workers openly derided King's commitment to nonviolence and black-white alliances. John Lewis, who had once reflected SNCC's mood, was now caught between SNCC's remaining proponents of Gandhian-Christian nonviolence and the growing number of staff members influenced by Malcolm X, the black nationalist leader who was assassinated in New York in February, shortly after he spoke to Alabama students and voting rights proponents.

To support the Alabama campaign, I joined sympathy demonstrations at the federal building in downtown Los Angeles, although I realized that such protests were unlikely to get the attention of President Lyndon Johnson and other federal officials. With a white activist who had worked in SNCC's project in Laurel, Mississippi, I staged an impromptu sit-in in the lobby of the building. We succeeded in briefly closing the building, but our main accomplishment was to assuage our guilt about not joining the march to Alabama's capitol in Montgomery.

Although N-VAC remained active during the spring and summer of 1965 and achieved some breakthroughs in its campaign against employment discrimination, the group was increasingly split along the same racial, class, and ideological lines that were beginning to tear SNCC apart. Even some white members of the group were sympathetic to the ideas of Malcolm X, but N-VAC's interracialism was increasingly difficult to maintain as black nationalist sentiments gained increasing support.

Opposition to the Johnson administration's escalation of the war in Vietnam was an issue that united all N-VAC members, although some felt it should not detract from racial concerns. My growing involvement in the antiwar movement was partly fueled by the likelihood that I would be drafted into the military. In May 1965 I attended a teach-in at the University of California's Berkeley campus on the Vietnam War and heard Bob Moses speak out against the war. He compared the lack of public concern about the recent death of Alabama black protester Jimmy Lee Jackson to the outpouring of national concern over the subsequent killing of a white civil rights activist, the Reverend James Reeb. Insisting that most white Americans cared little about the lives of nonwhites, Moses remarked that "you've got to learn from the South if you're going to do anything about this country in relation to Vietnam."

Perhaps sensing that my skills were ill-suited to the difficult task of community organizing, I began writing occasional articles for the *Los Angeles Free Press*, a newly established "underground" weekly. Political journalism allowed me to be a curious observer as well

as a participant in the California political world. My first article was a profile of N-VAC's Woody Coleman that began with his bold forecast: "I'm looking for a bloodbath this summer. We're going to get tired of being peaceful and nonviolent without getting anything." Woody described N-VAC as a "mean and nasty organization" that was the political counterpart of the Nation of Islam. The article concluded with another provocative prediction: "We won't get a solution until we put enough pressure, until the politicians realize that there's not going to be any peace until the Negroes get their freedom. The movement will probably come to bloodshed. We've tried enough nonviolence and seen that it doesn't work."

During the next two years, I would combine activism with writings that appeared in the underground press and New Left periodicals, both of which sought to bridge the widening chasm between white leftists and their black counterparts. Unable to satisfy my desire to join SNCC's staff, I found that political journalism in Los Angeles could be almost as intense as covering SNCC's efforts in the South. The distinction between northern and southern activism decreased as the southern civil rights efforts became part of a national black freedom struggle.

Early in August 1965 President Johnson signed the landmark Voting Rights Act with King and other national civil rights leaders attending the ceremony. For those affiliated with N-VAC and SNCC, however, the freedom struggle was far from over. Just a few days after the signing, an unprecedented explosion of racial violence engulfed south-central Los Angeles. The press referred to the Watts "riot," and the violence and looting was indeed chaotic, but I also witnessed an insurgency that briefly transformed large sections of Los Angeles into liberated zones of the black freedom struggle. Many residents were proud that they had overcome their fear of the city's police. Standing outside N-VAC's office on Central Avenue, I struggled to make sense of the mass rebellion that made our nonviolent, interracial militancy seem so insignificant.

N-VAC members sympathized with the angry black residents in the streets, but we refrained from joining in the arson and looting. A few of us organized a patrol to assist injured people unable to get to hospitals. While on a rescue mission, we had a violent clash with police who beat me and two others with their billy clubs. I felt fortunate to have survived, given that many other residents became "justifiable homicide" victims after similar encounters with police.

When King rushed to Watts in an attempt to stem the violence, many black residents reacted with indifference and even hostility. King explained to reporters that similar violent outbreaks would occur elsewhere unless programs were developed to confront the "economic deprivation, racial isolation, inadequate housing and general despair of thousands of Negroes teeming in Northern and Western ghettoes." After King's visit, my appreciation of his role increased as he made clear that his objectives extended beyond civil rights reform. Within a year, he would move to a Chicago slum and launch new protest campaigns focused on the kind of urban issues that N-VAC confronted.

During the summer of 1966, I reconnected with Stokely Carmichael following his election as SNCC's chair, replacing John Lewis. By then Stokely had left the Mississippi staff to direct a new project in rural central Alabama. Working with grassroots leaders such as John Hulett, Stokely, along with his SNCC colleagues Bob Mants, Scott B. Smith, Willie Vaugn, and Judy Richardson, helped to organize the Lowndes County Freedom Organization. The new group adopted the black panther as its symbol. Bouyed by the rapid emergence of the "Black Panther Party," Stokely, as SNCC's spokesperson, displayed on a larger stage the charisma I had seen at the 1963 NSA meeting.

When he took part in the Mississippi voting rights march held after the wounding of James Meredith in June 1966, Stokely used the occasion to popularize the "Black Power" slogan—a shortened version of the Lowndes County movement's goal of "Black Power for Black People." Stokely's rise to prominence came not only at the expense of John Lewis but also at the

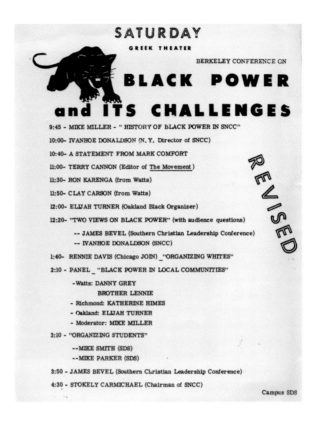

expense of King, who served as Stokely's foil for public debates about the Black Power slogan. When Stokely came to Los Angeles to speak at a well-attended rally in Watts, he received a much more enthusiastic response than King had received a year earlier.

My initial enthusiasm for the Black Power slogan was tempered by my awareness that Stokely's calls for black unity were accompanied by increasing internal divisions within SNCC, N-VAC, and many black communities. I was also concerned that Stokely's celebrity was a departure from SNCC's former emphasis on grassroots organizing rather than speech making. Although I still admired Stokely's commitment and courage, he seemed to be competing for prominence with other militant leaders, including black nationalists such as Ron (later Maulana) Karenga, the subject of one of my *Free Press* pieces.

In November 1966, Stokely and I both spoke at a Black Power Conference held at the Greek Theater on the Berkeley campus. Identified on the program as "from Watts" I was actually more a journalist than a community organizer. I realized that my function at the Berkeley rally was to warm up the audience for the person they really wanted to hear. I had already become uneasy with the antiwhite tone associated with the Black Power phenomenon, and found it difficult to reconcile the new racial militancy with my multiracial circle of activist friends and my growing involvement in the antiwar movement. Although Stokely was the nation's most influential Black Power advocate, he was himself torn between his roots in interracial socialist activism and his pursuit of Pan-African unity. His Berkeley audience was mostly white, and, after his speech, Stokely and I spent the evening in San Francisco's Haight-Ashbury neighborhood at an interracial party of movement veterans.

As SNCC's southern organizing efforts gave way to the Black Power militancy of the late 1960s, I gradually lost touch with the sense of discovery I felt at the March on Washington. The disintegration of SNCC's organizing efforts coincided with my realization that not all SNCC staff members fit the romanticized image I had created for them. Although I continued to be attracted to the ideal of bottom-up organizing that enabled oppressed people to shape their own destiny, I realized how difficult it was to overcome the freedom struggle's internal problems—especially racial tensions, anger caused by frustration, and growing competition for ideological dominance.

After graduating from UCLA in June 1967, I received my military induction orders and decided to leave the United States along with my wife, Susan—a Jewish woman I had met through mutual friends in SNCC and N-VAC. While applying for permission to immigrate to Canada, we traveled in Europe and for a brief time in Morocco. We had only modest savings but managed to survive on less than ten dollars per day. While in southern Spain, however, we were forced by Susan's undiagnosed diabetes to return to the United States in March 1968, shortly before I heard the shocking news of King's assassination.

After contacting a draft lawyer, I found work as a computer programmer on the UCLA campus. Although I attended campus antiwar rallies and meetings to discuss the need for a black studies program, my job and family (a son arrived in the fall of 1969) occupied my time, and I did not resume my journalism or join any political organization. I remained curious about the movement, however, and this curiosity stimulated a broader desire to know more about how the modern black freedom struggle fit into African American history.

While continuing to work as a computer programmer, I began auditing a new UCLA course on American race relations—the first of the courses that were offered in the aftermath of King's death. As one of a small number of black college graduates on campus, I was recruited by Professor Gary Nash to be an informal teaching assistant, leading a section of the course devoted to black political thought. Despite my earlier feelings of being an outsider, I knew more than most academics and much more than most students about recent developments in African American history. Political activism had once drawn me away from my undergraduate classes; now it provided an impetus to become a historian.

By the time I began graduate school in history in the fall of 1969, there were few remaining signs of the movement I had discovered in 1963. N-VAC no longer existed, although its legacy was evident in the expanded economic opportunities available to black residents. Operation Bootstrap, founded by Robert Hall, provided much-needed jobs (one of its enterprises produced the first commercial black dolls). The groups that supplanted N-VAC included the Black Panther Party and Maulana Karenga's US organization. The two groups engaged in a bitter conflict that culminated in the killing of two Panthers in a building not far from my office on the UCLA campus. That black militants could kill other black militants confirmed my doubts about the shift from grassroots organizing to "blacker than thou" competition among groups and leaders determined to raise the consciousness of the black masses.

SNCC also declined as the tumultuous decade of the 1960s ended. After the departure of nearly all of its most effective organizers, SNCC's few remaining staff members engaged in destructive ideological battles that even the ever-vigilant FBI Counterintelligence Program (COINTELPRO) found unworthy of surveillance. A group that had once emphasized building the leadership capabilities of grassroots leaders had become a group of self-appointed leaders vainly seeking a following. When I decided to make SNCC the subject of my doctoral research, my goal was to understand how and why this remarkable group came apart as well as the reasons it came together.

Stokely had quickly gone from notoriety to obscurity after joining forces with the Black Panther Party for Self-Defense, the California-based group that had supplanted SNCC as the most dynamic organization in the black freedom struggle. Although the Black Panthers borrowed its name from SNCC's Lowndes County project, its military-style hierarchical organization had little in common with SNCC's decentralized decision-making process. After a brief alliance of the Black Panthers and SNCC splintered during 1968, Stokely's former SNCC colleagues expelled him when he decided to remain with the Panthers. Stokely was then forced out of the Panthers in large measure because of his criticisms of their ties to white radicals.

Becoming a disciple of deposed Ghanaian leader Kwame Nkrumah, Stokely moved to Guinea where he worked closely with the exiled Nkrumah and with Guinea's leader Guinean Ahmed Sékou Touré (Stokely later adopted the name Kwame Turé). As part of my research for a dissertation (and later a book) about SNCC, I interviewed Stokely on several occasions during his visits to the United States (and also invited him to lecture to my students after becoming a professor at Stanford). I would always see him as the gifted leader who had introduced me to SNCC but found it difficult to understand his transformation from Mississippi organizer to Pan-African ideologue. Although I admired his enduring dedication to the effort to build

the All African Peoples Revolutionary Party, I was not surprised that it attracted the support of only a few of his former SNCC colleagues.

I also interviewed John Lewis in the early 1970s. By then John had become director of the Atlanta-based Voter Education Project, formed to increase the number of black registered voters in the South and envisioning a future in which "hands that once picked cotton could now pick a president." He would go on to a successful political career, first as associate director of the volunteer agency, Action, in the Jimmy Carter administration, then as an Atlanta city councilman, and still later as a U. S. Congressman representing a district in Atlanta. His emergence as a nationally prominent, black voice of moral integrity would always be rooted in his earlier role as SNCC's spokesperson at the March on Washington.

He remained somewhat bitter about his unseating as SNCC's chair by Stokely's supporters in 1966, but his dismay was mainly focused on SNCC's subsequent inability to sustain its projects in the South. "To have a program is one thing, to have a sort of speech-making public relations thing is another," he told me in 1972. Recounting the last-minute negotiations over his March on Washington speech, he acknowledged feeling angry "that someone would tell me what to say and what should be deleted." But he and many others who demonstrated in front of the Lincoln Memorial must have felt a special satisfaction in 2009 when these former demonstrators celebrated the inauguration of Barack Obama at the other end of the Washington Mall. A month after the inauguration, John and I were members of a congressional delegation to India to commemorate the fiftieth anniversary of King's pilgrimage to the land of Gandhi—the inspiration for both King and the younger Gandhians in James Lawson's Nashville workshop.

Because Bob Moses was still in Africa when I completed my study—published by Harvard University Press as *In Struggle: SNCC and the Black Awakening of the 1960s*—I was not able to interview him until after the book's publication in 1981. Yet, although I was almost two decades removed from the naïve teenager I had been when I first heard him speak, my two-day interview deepened my understanding of the sources of SNCC's distinctive organizing techniques. Bob insisted that long-time SNCC advisor Ella Baker had been his inspiration. Because of my earlier interview with Baker, whose career as an organizer extended back to the 1930s, and my interviews with many others influenced by her, I realized that Bob was not engaging in false modesty. Grassroots organizing had always been an essential aspect of the African American freedom struggle, which began when Africans first resisted slavery and did not end with the passage of national civil rights legislation. Bob's own activism has continued with his current Algebra Project, which seeks to empower poorly educated black people in Mississippi and elsewhere to achieve better educational opportunities.

Bob Moses and Ella Baker are exemplars of an ideal that remains at the center of my worldview. Their principles have affected my teaching and writing as well as my political activism. Their work as organizers offers guidance to anyone seeking to overcome oppression without creating new kinds of dependence. SNCC's slogan, "Our job is to work ourselves out of a job," reflects their notion of developing self-reliant grassroots leaders. SNCC's best organizers sought to build truly democratic movements and institutions in which all people participate equally in decisions affecting their destiny. Teachers influenced by SNCC recognized that their role is to liberate students rather than prepare them for subordinate roles in a world they cannot shape.

Four years after *In Struggle* was published and more than two decades after the March on Washington, Coretta Scott King unexpectedly asked me to assemble and edit her late husband's papers. My admiration for SNCC made me an unlikely choice for this role, but the passage of years had deepened my understanding of the man who once seemed the antithesis of SNCC's bottom-up ethos. Yet, even after I accepted Coretta's invitation, I continued for a time to downplay King's

historical significance. At a 1986 conference on Martin Luther King held in Washington and sponsored by the United States Capitol Historical Society, I reiterated my view that "if King had never lived, the black struggle would have followed a course of development similar to the one it did." I insisted that civil rights reforms would have been achieved "without King's leadership," although I went on to suggest that without King this would have occurred "perhaps not as quickly and certainly not as peacefully or with as universal a significance."

During the 1960s, my own youthful impatience and a degree of arrogance led me to question King's firm commitment to integration and nonviolence in the face of white racist attacks. But my realization that the Black Power movement failed to achieve much power and even failed to achieve much racial unity has fostered a greater degree of humility in my assessments of King's alternative course. For me, King became wiser as I became older. My changing views of him have been affected not only by my personal experiences, but also by the unique opportunity I have had to study both the black movement's foremost statesman and its impetuous foot soldiers.

In the years since the March on Washington, I have often returned to the Mall and have found myself reflecting on how little I knew as a nineteen-year-old student. Having now studied many thousands of King-related documents, I have gained an appreciation for his unique role in the freedom struggle. Just as SNCC's organizing projects were essential to the growth of the southern mass movement, so too was King's visionary leadership essential. Indeed, it was one of my interviews with Stokely that clarified the relationship between SNCC's organizing efforts and King's prophetic role. "People loved King," Stokely explained. "I've seen people in the South climb over each other just to say, 'I touched him! I touched him! . . . I'm even talking about the young. The old people had more love and respect. They even saw him like a God. These were the people we were working with and I had to follow in his footsteps when I went in there. The people didn't know what was SNCC. They just said, 'You one of Dr. King's men?' 'Yes, ma'am, I am.'"

My conversations with King's relatives and SCLC associates have brought me ever closer to the man I was only able to see from a distance. My work on the multivolume edition of *The Papers of Martin Luther King, Jr.* has embedded his words into my memory. I learned of King's own deep respect for the grassroots activists who made possible the Montgomery bus boycott—"I want you to know that if M. L. King had never been born this movement would have taken place," he once remarked at a Montgomery mass meeting. He appreciated the crucial importance of Fred Shuttlesworth and the Children's Crusade in transforming his pending defeat in Birmingham into a magnificent victory.

Studying King's papers has also shed light on the March on Washington by allowing me to see what I missed. I have used King's writings to describe the march from his perspective rather than mine and in 1998 published a compilation of his autobiographical writings —titled *The Autobiography of Martin Luther King, Jr.*—that included a chapter about the march. More than three decades after the event, I was able to tell the story of King's impromptu decision to depart from the text that he had finished in the early morning hours preceding the march.

King's prepared text was addressed to the "architects of our republic" who signed a "promissory note to which every American was to fall heir. This note was a promise that all men, yes, black men as well as white men, would be guaranteed the unalienable rights of 'Life, Liberty and the pursuit of Happiness.'" King's dialogue with the nation's founders was an expression of his singular prophetic role, but I am grateful that King had the vision to understand that white Americans needed more than a blunt reminder that the nation had "given the Negro people a bad check, a check which has come back marked 'insufficient.'"

Seeing the march from King's perspective, I understood that King refused to allow his audience to "wallow in the valley of despair." I realized that King made a momentous decision while I was desperately seeking a ride from the march. "The audience's response was wonderful that day, and all of a sudden this thing came to me," King remembered thinking as he reached the end of his prepared text. He remembered a phrase from the speech he had delivered the previous June at Detroit's Cobo Hall. "I had used it many times before and I just felt that I wanted to use it here. I don't know why. I hadn't thought about it before the speech. I used the phrase, and at that point I just turned aside from the manuscript altogether and didn't come back to it."

King often gave us hope during those times when the outcome of the black freedom struggle was uncertain. "I still have a dream," he proclaimed. "It is a dream deeply rooted in the American dream. I have a dream that one day this nation will rise up and live out the meaning of its creed—we hold these truths to be self-evident that all men are created equal."

During the remaining years of his life, there were many times when King suspected that his dream was turning into a nightmare. Late in his life, unable to end the Vietnam war and in the midst of the floundering Poor People's Campaign, he described life as "a continual story of shattered dreams." Although many of us in the black freedom struggle also became discouraged, we depended on King to remind us that "we, as a people, will get to the promised land."

At the end of his life, King had many reasons to be discouraged as he realized that his ambitious dreams would not be realized. Nonetheless, his final "Mountain Top" speech in Memphis reiterated his appreciation that God had allowed him to participate in history's greatest freedom struggle. He reminded black Americans that their freedom struggle was connected to the anticolonial struggles occurring throughout the world. "Something is happening in our world," he told Memphis sanitation workers. "The masses of people are rising up. And wherever they are assembled today, whether they are in Johannesburg, South Africa; Nairobi, Kenya; Accra, Ghana; New York City; Atlanta, Georgia; Jackson, Mississippi; or Memphis, Tennessee, the cry is always the same: 'We want to be free.'"

The Photographers

Interviews and Biographies

Tamio Wakayama

Tamio Wakayama was born on April 3, 1941, a few months before the outbreak of the Pacific War. He and his family were part of the community of some twenty-two thousand Japanese Canadians (Nikkei) living along the coast of British Columbia who were declared enemy aliens and placed in remote internment camps for the war years. After the war, the internees were faced with the choice of being deported to Japan or else settling east of the Rockies. Wakayama's family went east and settled in Chatham, a farming town in southern Ontario. Chatham was once the terminus of the Underground Railway, so many of Wakayama's boyhood friends were Afro-Canadian descendants of runaway slaves.

As Wakayama explains, the central challenge of his life was coming to terms with the internment and the debilitating effects of the postwar racism. The healing process began in the fall of 1963 when, instead of returning to finish his university education, he drove south and became part of the American Civil Rights Movement. After working as a volunteer janitor and driver for the Student Nonviolent Coordinating Committee (SNCC), he was accepted as a staff member of the Atlanta office. In the following year he managed the darkroom for the Southern Documentary Project, which was part of the Freedom Summer '64 campaign and, at the end of summer, he took over as the SNCC field photographer in Mississippi.

At the end of 1964, Wakayama returned to Canada and assisted the Toronto-based Student Union for Peace Action (SUPA) in organizing in behalf of the Civil Rights Movement. He also participated in a photographic tour of various SUPA-sponsored organizing projects and photographed for the Company of Young Canadians (modelled on the American VISTA program). In 1971 Wakayama spent a year in Japan, a life-altering experience which led him to reconnect with his roots. He eventually moved from Toronto to Vancouver and became part of the reawakening Nikkei community that had grown around the prewar settlement of Little Tokyo. In 1975 he became the curator/director of the Japanese Canadian Centennial Project, which two years later produced A Dream of Riches, a monumental exhibit on the one-hundred-year-old history of the Nikkei that has been seen in over forty venues in

I didn't go south with any set plan like I'm going to join this wonderful movement. Essentially, I'm just this kid from small-town Chatham. I said, "Mom, I've worked hard all summer, I just want a little vacation in the States before going back to finish my final year of college." But in another way, leaving was huge, absolutely huge. I was one of the early college dropouts from a small town in a very white community, to which is added the rigors of Japanese parents who didn't put up with much nonsense. And all this would not have been possible if my father hadn't died, 'cause I would have had to answer to him. And I'm almost certain that had he been around, I wouldn't have done it.

I left early September [of 1963], and I just had this sense of—I've got to check out this thing that's compelling my interest. So I drove down, and I'd been there a couple of days already, sleeping in my car, and as my wife, Mayu, would attest, I am a lousy tourist. So I'd gotten to Nashville, took a tour of the stately capitol buildings and was bored, 'cause if you've seen one stately building you've seen them all. I said, jeez, what the hell am I doing here? Maybe I should go back. And that's when the news bulletin came on my radio, in my Beetle. I checked my maps and saw Birmingham was about a two-hundred-mile straight drive south, so I went. I'm acting on instinct primarily. This incredible tragedy happened in Birmingham, a bomb exploded in a Baptist church, in the basement where there's a Bible study class going on. Four young girls have died; scores of others are injured. Huge news! And it was like a star [appeared] over Birmingham, saying: Follow it. I followed it. And tragic as that event was, for me, I hate to say this, it was a gift because it drew me into the movement.

I landed [in Birmingham] after getting lost in a residential area, and was surrounded by a bunch of [black] kids who were angry and ready to retaliate in some way. I got out [of the car], and they were ready to do heavy damage, except they stopped for a minute—hey, what is this guy? He ain't white, he ain't the enemy, but he ain't black, so I leapt in. I said, "Excuse me, I'm a student from Canada, and I'm trying to get to the YMCA. I'm going to vacation in Mexico, and I just got lost. I heard about this terrible bombing, and I want you to know how sorry I am that this awful thing's happened. But I'd appreciate it if you could give me directions." So that cooled them, and they said: Y'all go down here and do this, and they added, "But you be careful going there, boy, because this is no night for you to be wandering by yourself in Birmingham." I said, "Thanks," and so I found my way into Birmingham.

Since I'd been driving all day, I was hungry and I needed a rest stop. I was looking for one, but it was really a strange atmosphere 'cause, I mean, this urban setting, on [a] pleasantly warm, breezy, southern fall night was practically deserted. I looked around, there's hardly anybody on the street. I go by theaters and it's dark. But I spot this place. I whip around and park behind this pickup truck, and I see it's got Dixie flags pinioned all over the back and these banners, "Keep America White," or "Keep the South White." I walk in. It's one of those ubiquitous barbecue shacks that permeate the South, and it's a black establishment. There are about six black men sitting there. They're *big*, and they look pretty mean to me [chuckles]. I sit at the counter, and I literally could feel those eyes boring into my back like, "Who the fuck is this guy?" So I order coffee and a plate of ribs and the counter helper, a young kid, is checking me out. I see him staring at my package of red Du Maurier cigarettes. I said, "They're Canadian. It's a different kind of tobacco. Try one. See how you like it." He took one, and he said, "They are different. I'm not sure I like it," but that broke the ice.

Then the owner comes over. He's six, seven years older than me, light-skinned. I start talking to him, and I said, "I'm from Canada, I'm a student and when I saw what was happening with the Civil Rights Movement, it really grabbed me. I just had to see for myself what all this business is." He said, "Oh, yeah, okay," and then he began to tell me what it was like to be black in the Deep South. And it was this horrific story about where at any moment if you're in Birmingham or in Mississippi and you aren't careful, you could be, at the very least, humiliated, and, at the very worst, lynched. I was just totally *aghast* at this tale, and then he says, "Well, I sure do appreciate y'all coming down to see what it's all about. But I think you should get back in your little car and go home, and tell your people up in Canada that it's all real, what's happening here. All the beatings, all the bombings, all the jailings and fire hoses and them lynchings, it's all real, my man. But you be careful leaving, 'cause you see that truck you parked behind?" I said, "Yes, sir." He said, "Well, that's probably the Klan. They're keeping an eye on us 'cause we're about the only place open in Birmingham tonight."

I thanked him profusely for the history lesson and the *great* ribs, 'cause they were very tasty. But before I left, I managed to get one vital piece of information. Okay, obviously, this was a big event, and civil rights leaders would be converging, and where would that be happening? He said, "The movement headquarters is the A.G. Gaston Motel." And where is that? So I had that information, and I did, in fact, find the YMCA. I checked in and spent the night. The next morning I asked some people at the Y how to get to the Gaston Motel. And I learned A. G. Gaston was a highly successful [black] businessman in Birmingham and probably, at that time, one of the few millionaires; and his motel—the only desegregated facility in the city—became the de facto headquarters of the movement because leaders when they came to town would stay there.

So that's where I went. I walked into the lobby. There's a lot of people there, and most of them are young, and I can relate 'cause they're my age and they're dressed in dungarees. The young people, I later learned, were primarily SNCC field workers, and I happened to see John Lewis. I go over and I said, "Mr. Lewis, I just want you to know that of all the people I heard on the March on Washington, I remember being most affected by your words." It was true, because I

remember being carried away by the soaring oratory of Martin Luther King's dream speech. But because it was so mellifluous and grand, you knew it was oratory. But then I see John Lewis, head of this organization called the Student Nonviolent Coordinating Committee. I never heard of them before and he gets up. He has none of the precise diction of the other speakers, but what he's saying is real. I can feel the righteous anger in there, the guy's pissed off, and he's telling it like it is. He's saying—there's a party of Democrats and Republicans. Where is my party? Where's the party of justice?[1] I said, Yeah, you're right.

So I expressed all this to John, and I told him my genesis in coming. We talked and I was quite taken that he's taking the time to listen and we're exchanging our lives to some extent. At the end of it, he says, "You're welcome to come to Atlanta and check out SNCC headquarters, for which I'm the chair." I said, "Thank you very much," and he says, "Oh, and you want to meet some other people," so he introduced me to Julian Bond and a few others. I don't remember whether Danny [Lyon] was there, but he showed up eventually 'cause he was one of the people I drove to Atlanta. So that was the beginning.

After attending the funeral [for the girls], I took John up on his offer, and I said, "I am going to go to Atlanta, and I have an empty car. It's small but if anybody wants a ride, they're welcome." So I took James Forman, the executive secretary of SNCC, Danny [Lyon], and Julian Bond; so essentially I had a good part of the leadership of this major civil rights organization in my car that day, driving to Atlanta in a used 1958 Volkswagen Beetle. So I'm driving, and this is the first time I've had this many people in my car, and Forman's a big man. We're on this two-lane highway, and I'm crawling behind this truck who is going like ridiculously slow, and I said, screw this, I've gotta pass this guy. I shifted and I whip around and there's a semi coming down on the opposite lane. I figure I've got plenty of time, but I didn't realize what the addition of three other bodies and some five hundred pounds would do to the car. I tromped on the gas and it wasn't the usual zoom. The Beetle didn't have much to begin with, but with the extra weight it was like, Holy Christ, what will I do? I just managed to zip by the truck in front of me and the semi comes whizzing by. I'm getting angry honks from the truck and we just barely make it; everybody's going, phew. I think, oh, yeah, that would have been a great start to my entrance to the South, wipe out the leadership of a civil rights organization. Good going.

From there, well, my involvement with SNCC just grew. I mean, I literally just dropped onto their doorstep one day, and when I met the staff the following morning, they were young like me, and a fairly even mixture of black and white students from various parts of the South. I was the only Asian. But my presence wasn't particularly startling because they were used to all kinds of people drifting into their headquarters. So as far as I was concerned and I guess everybody else, I was there to check things out. But I tried to be as useful as possible. And SNCC was the youngest and poorest of the main Civil Rights Movement [organizations], so my Beetle, which I used to chauffeur people and to deliver what needed to be delivered or picked up, was a huge asset. So I wormed my way in and gradually got to be part of a community environment.

And SNCC at this time had this massive campaign to desegregate the restaurants in the downtown, and so the Atlanta jail was filling up with sit-in demonstrators, a good number of which were SNCC office staff. Since the staff knew they were going to carry on and more bodies were needed, it was decided to hold a mass rally on the nearby black campuses of Spelman and Morehouse colleges. The rally was planned, but there was nobody left in our office to produce the advertisement material to get the people out. So I went down. I'd never done any of this before, and I figured, let's see what we can do. I found this powerful image Forman had taken earlier in the campaign. It was a tight headshot of a Klansman, fat cheeks,

staring, growling out a restaurant window. He's in full regalia, white sheet, pointed cap. And it was like, wow, look at that! I took that image and figured out how to work the Varityper, which was this headline-producing machine. It was just rotate and click, and I had big captions, "The face of Atlanta. Help change it," and the rally particulars underneath. Sandwiched between the text was the image of the Klansman. So that was circulated around campus. We had a huge turnout, and everybody loved the poster. And Danny [Lyon] looked at it and said, "Wow, that's some boss stuff. You ought to try your hand with photography, and I'll even lend you one of my spare Nikons," which he did, and that is essentially how I got to be in photography. And, of course, I will always be grateful to Danny for that.

So my work began to increase within SNCC. I was starting to work more on *The Student Voice*, their publication, helping with layout and proofreading—and that was like the movement at that time. You arrived, you used whatever skills and assets [you had], and you contributed. It was also a time when it didn't matter that you didn't know a particular skill like running an AB Dick machine printing press or operating a darkroom. It was like, we're young, we are the movement, and we learn as we go along. And we had the confidence that we could just about do anything we wanted, 'cause we were on the side of a good cause. So I was slowly getting entrenched in SNCC, and at some point it became obvious I was not just a visitor. But it wasn't until about probably month and a half that I'd been with SNCC that I had the temerity to speak up at a staff meeting. I piped up with, I said, "Look, I've got limited resources to maintain me and my car. But I'm more than happy to use any of that for SNCC business, but I think people are starting to take advantage. They're asking me to take them to the hairdresser or to pick up a six-pack, so I'd like people to be a bit more respectful of me." And that was cool, and after that, Forman, the executive, decided to put me on the SNCC payroll, with a modest amount of expenses for my car, which was great because the money I'd earned in the summer job was just about used up. Plus now I was part of SNCC and this incredible movement that was transforming the face of America and would go on to affect the entire world. I remember, it was one of the proudest moments of my young life.

Was SNCC's concept of nonviolence ever discussed with you?

No, there was never any indoctrination into a specific philosophy. SNCC wasn't into that. They weren't missionaries. As long as you worked and were sincere and you weren't going to be a pain in the ass, it was cool. You became a part of SNCC, and there was this sense that we were all together at a really important time in history. Yeah, there was a sense pervading that period that not only were we a part of history, but we were history itself. Like we were the vanguard of this whole new, bright millennium. It may have been tremendously naïve, but there was that underlying sense of that, and it was a unique and passionate time of our young lives. I can remember Julian [Bond] coming up after I'd moved to Toronto, a number of years later after we'd both left—well, after SNCC had died for all intents and purposes. He'd come up for various Canadian Broadcasting Corporation public affair shows that wanted him as a guest, so he called me up and we went to dinner, and in this great voice, "You know, Wakayama," he always called me Wakayama, "you know, man," he says, "I don't think I can ever put out as much as I put out in those days. It was just unbelievable." Yeah, so that was the temper of the times.

Did you participate in the efforts to desegregate Atlanta restaurants?

Well, I remember ferrying people back and forth from various sit-ins. A lot of times I'd go with Danny, but I was wary of actually joining in and getting arrested, because I was afraid I would be deported 'cause I'm not an American citizen. But [one time] I did go with Danny and some SNCC workers to Loeb's Restaurant, which was one of the more upscale restaurants in downtown Atlanta. Anyway, we sit around the counter

and out comes Loeb, the owner, and he's pissed off. He says, "People, get out of my restaurant. You're destroying my business." And Danny Lyon goes ballistic. He says, "Loeb, how can you do this? You're a Jew like me. Don't you remember the camps? You're acting like the goddamn Nazi!" And wow, that's the only time I saw Danny lose his photographic cool, but I remember that very clearly.

And that wild scene suddenly reminded me of that moment I turned on the TV and saw a sit-in at some lunch counter in Danville, Virginia. This was before I went south, and this was one of the moments that inspired me to go. I remember there was like maybe seven, eight young people like myself, both black and white, and they sat there quite calmly. And the mob around them, the owners, hurled abuse at them, "Get out, you fuckin' niggers," that usual litany. Then they'd crack eggs over their heads and anoint them with coffee and Coke. And the more aggressive ones would throw them on the ground. They'd quietly pick [themselves] up, didn't shout back. They didn't look particularly disturbed. With a great deal of dignity, [they] just went back and sat at the counter. That blew me away. That totally blew me away. And I sensed then that I was connected [to these people] in some deep and yet still unnamed, unidentified part of me.

Can you name that part of you that felt connected to the demonstrators?

No, I don't have a name for it, but as you grow up as a black or as a Jap in this country, you know with all the things you have to deal with as a child growing up in a hostile and dominant white world that a good part of your inner being, your sense of self, is destroyed. For blacks, it's like I'm a slave or I'm a descendent of slaves. I'm this downtrodden, no-good nigger. I'm this kind of not-quite human life form. For me, I'm a Jap. I'm the enemy. I'm this yellow, sexless, savage beast that anyone could spit on. And you've gotta be careful 'cause that [stereotype] can destroy your inner being. So the first stage of liberation is you've gotta get rid of all that shit, and you've got to be able to say, "I refuse.

I'm not what they are saying. I'm a human being. I have value, and I'm proud of what I am, and I'm proud of my history." That's what you've got to work through, and that was the essence of the struggle of those young people in Danville, and that has been the essence of my struggle, and of my art, my photography, throughout my life.

Note

1. John Lewis's actual words were: "What political leader here can stand up and say 'My party is the party of principles'? The party of Kennedy is also the party of Eastland. The party of Javits is also the party of Goldwater. Where is our party?"

Herbert Randall

Herbert Eugene Randall, Jr., was born on December 16, 1936, in the Bronx and is of Shinnecock Indian, African American, and West Indian ancestry. He studied photography under Harold Feinstein in 1957, and from 1958 to 1966 worked as a freelance photographer, publishing with the Associated Press, United Press International, and Black Star. Randall also was a founding member of the Kamoinge Workshop, a forum formed by African American photographers in New York City in 1963 to address the underrepresentation of black photographers in the art world and to encourage major media outlets to present African American people and culture in a more authentic, complex, and compassionate manner.

In 1964, Sandy Leigh, director of Mississippi Freedom Summer's Hattiesburg project, invited Randall to document the project and its impact in Hattiesburg. Randall spent the summer photographing area activities such as Freedom Schools, voter registration, and the Mississippi Freedom Democratic Party campaign. His photos were developed in SNCC's Atlanta darkroom by Tamio Wakayama, and five images were published that summer. The bloodied image of Rabbi Arthur Lelyveld, a short-term summer volunteer and head of Cleveland's Fairmount Temple, received widespread distribution.

After the summer, Randall returned to New York and for the next three decades his movement photographs sat in a file at the Shinnecock Reservation in Southampton. In 1999, Randall donated eighteen hundred negatives to the archives of the University of Southern Mississippi in Hattiesburg, and over the ensuing two years, he and Bobs Tusa, the archivist at USM, compiled Faces of Freedom Summer, *published by the University of Alabama Press in 2001.* Faces *is the only record of a single town in the midst of the Civil Rights Movement in America.*

I applied for the John Hay Fellowship in 1963 [in New York], because I dearly liked to take some time to devote to photography. I did photography part-time, and I wanted to know what it felt like to have that luxury—luxury for me—just to work at photography. It didn't turn out that way, but that's why I applied. I don't remember *exactly* what I wrote to get it—a lot of bullshit, I think [laughs]. The title was "The New Negro"—I was gonna document the new Negro. But primarily I wanted a year to work at my craft. I found out in April of 1964 that I had received the fellowship and that enabled me to go to Mississippi.

How did Mississippi come onto the horizon?

I had a friend at the time, Julie Prettyman. She was running the New York SNCC office. My proposal for the fellowship stated that I needed to take photographs in the South, and Julie had read the proposal and said, "Herb, since you have to go to the South, SNCC has a summer program. Why don't you hook up with that?" I said, "Oh, wow, that might be a good idea." But I didn't ask her which part of the South. When she told me that it was in Mississippi, I said, "I'll go south, but that's insanity south!" I wasn't interested in getting killed over going to the South.

There was a meeting held at the Church Center, and Sandy Leigh, who was the project director for Hattiesburg, [Mississippi], was up recruiting people—potential volunteers. Julie called me and said, "Why don't you just go to the meeting? I know you don't want to go, but see what he has to say." I went and Sandy spoke, and after the meeting he for some reason asked if I were going to Mississippi or thinking [of it]. I said, "I had thought about it, but I'm not into going to Mississippi." Anyhow, he was in New York for a week or so and we hung out and spoke a lot, [and] I thought, "I could work with this guy." I thought [more] about it, and then decided I would go.

What made him convince you?

Sandy made everything sound simple, but I think it was more my feeling this is somebody I could work with. I mean, he said, "Why don't you just come and document my program—that's all you have to do. You do it the way you want to do it." I said, "That sounds good to me." Anyhow, I knew the summer program was important, that was not a question to me. If you could teach kids how to become more productive, if you could help register people to vote, if you could in any

way help in that sense, I mean, it's a no-brainer. But it's Mississippi in 1964, so that [was a] big consideration.

I sense that you're somewhat reluctant to talk about the summer. Is this hard for you?

Certainly reliving Mississippi is hard for me, but it's interesting [as well]. I was at Miami University a couple of years ago, and I was talking to students [about the summer]. And one of the professors asked if I would like to look at what they were doing with a group she had. Some of her students were reenacting the letters and the memos [of the volunteers] and some of the things that happened at the training session in Ohio. I was sitting there listening to it, and all of a sudden I just broke out and started crying—I mean, it was uncontrollable. So I'm saying [to myself], "What the hell is this about?" not particularly at the time, but I mean, they were reenacting some of the things that happened in Ohio. And I think what it was is that during that summer I didn't have time—I mean, it was continuous; day by day somebody [was] threatening [you] in some kind of way, or somebody would come in and say, "Oh, that guy's there with the pickup truck with the shotguns in the back again." And you didn't have time to digest that because something is happening somewhere else, something horrible. And two months of this—and when you leave Mississippi you have other things to do; you have a life to run. And I never really thought about a lot of the horror, and I guess all the horror came back in a condensed way because I never really had to deal with it.

I think you were called down to Washington DC before going south. Why was that?

Julie called me as I was preparing to go to Mississippi—Oxford, Ohio, first—and she said I needed to go to Washington DC. I said, "Why do I have to go to Washington DC?" She says, "Herb, don't ask. Just go, please." I said, "Okay." I went and I was supposed to see Marion Barry.[1] I wasn't a volunteer—I was going to photograph, and so that was one of the reasons I suspect I had to go see Marion Barry. Anyhow, I finally got to see Marion Barry, and he spoke as if he didn't know what the hell I wanted or who I was. He said I should go see Julian Bond, and whatever Julian said was fine with him. I said, "Well, that's fine." So someone in the office said Julian was a couple of blocks away at a restaurant. I had never met Julian before, but I had some idea of what he looked like. I saw a family there [at the restaurant], and so I went up to the table and excused myself for interrupting their meal. But I told them I needed to see him and one thing led to another. He said he was finished with his meal, and I could walk him over to the auto repair place where his car was being serviced. So I told him Marion Barry had told me to see him, and he says, "What for?" I explained what I could explain, and he says, "Well, if you want to go, it's fine with me." And that was it. I did ask him, "What do you think is going to happen in Mississippi this summer?" He said, "There's gonna be a lot of people being killed."

A couple of weeks later, I was on my way to Oxford with other volunteers. We drove from New York City to Oxford, Ohio, and the day after we arrived Bob Moses was in a large auditorium, and he told us that three of the people who were in the first training session and who had gone to Mississippi were missing. Bob said they were probably dead, and this initiated my week at Oxford, Ohio. I understand the training session the first week was quite different, because it became more apparent, I mean the possibility existed of the danger, but when three people are missing and someone who knows Mississippi says they're dead in all probability, then it is no longer a theoretical thing. It's an actual fact, and you say, "Hey, I'm going down there next week, too."

Anyhow, we went through the training session. Some of the classes I went to, some I didn't. At the end of the week, most of the people went down to Mississippi by buses. For some reason or another I was told that I was going down by car. We were informed that the first group who went down were harassed. It was not only people in Mississippi who were harassing them, it was in all the southern states. It was almost as

if these volunteers were [seen as] coming to invade the southern states, and so the law enforcement people were harassing them throughout. So you not only had to be concerned about Mississippi, you had to be concerned about getting to Mississippi. In the car that I was to go to Mississippi in, there were six of us. The makeup was interesting: there was a white male, four white females, and myself [laughs]. This is not the way you want to go into Mississippi. And we were in a white foreign car with northern license plates. So we decided to go into Mississippi in daylight. We planned our trip; we figured about how long it would take to get there; and we left late one night.

I don't even remember how long it took us to get there, and we decided since I was odd man out in a matter of speaking, that at night I would sit in the passenger's seat in the front and during daylight I would be in the back covered over with a blanket or I'd lay down as best I could in the back seat. We left at night and got through Kentucky, and we were in some rural area in Kentucky, and we were really lost. So we pulled off the main road into a clearing to look at a map. Since it was at night, I was sitting in the front, in the passenger side. We pulled into this area, and there were no dome lights in the car because you would always unscrew the dome lights so you don't get out of a car in Mississippi or whatever, and have the lights go on because that makes you an easy target. Anyhow, since we had unloosened the dome light, I had a flashlight and the windows were partially open. The ladies were in the back, and I was looking at the map, and one of the ladies said, "There's a police car in the back." We collectively got quiet, and I remember thinking, Oh, my God, we haven't even made it to Mississippi and we're gonna get killed, or beaten, or put in jail.

I may have had the flashlight in my right hand, I don't remember, but I beamed down at the map on my lap, and I was staring down there. I just kept looking down. I didn't look around. It seems as though it was quiet forever, nobody spoke; we were just waiting for something to happen. Then I heard someone say, "Is there a problem?" It was the policeman. He said, "Are you folks broken down?" It wasn't threatening. It was just "what's wrong here?" Nobody said anything. I finally said, "We're lost." We needed to find whichever route we needed to be on, and I'm still not looking at him. All of a sudden, I saw a hand come through to the map. I still didn't look, and the hand pointed and the voice said, "You go here, you go up to," he was giving directions, but it didn't penetrate. I remember him saying, "Do you understand?" I said, "Oh, yes, yes." So he left, and then I turned around and saw the police car pulling off, and the driver said, "Okay, now, where do we go?" Nobody knew [laughs]. We all said, "Let's just get the hell out of here."

Anyhow, we got to Mississippi [in the] early daylight, which we had planned, and we had to stop in Jackson to check in, 'cause once you were in the state of Mississippi somebody had to know where you were. I'm talking about COFO.[2] So we stopped at the office on Lynch Street—I remember that street well, and I don't remember a damn thing [these days], but I remember the name of that street, Lynch Street, my God. I remember getting out of the car. I was a young man at the time, but I couldn't straighten up all the way. So we went into the office, and we all had to go to the bathroom, because everybody was trying to hold it because we didn't want to go to the bathrooms in Mississippi or anywhere else in those southern states. So we went to the bathroom, checked in, and then we went down to Hattiesburg. I was to stay in Hattiesburg. The rest were going to other parts of Mississippi, but all of the people stayed overnight just to rest. Sandy took me to the home of the Wilson family, where I stayed for the summer, and they showed me the room I could stay in.

I went to sleep and the next morning Doug Smith, [a] seventeen-year-old high school student who was the assistant director of the project in Hattiesburg, picked me up and took me back to the office on Mobile Street in Hattiesburg. On the way he said, "We had a shooting last night." Two of the cars of volunteers were shot into, and one of the cars happened to be the car that I had come to Mississippi in. So both of them

were disabled. So I got to Mobile Street, and those were the first photographs that I took—bullet holes in cars—and that was the beginning of my stay in Hattiesburg.

So then I had to make a decision as to what I was to photograph. I had to find out exactly what needed to be done, because when Sandy was in New York, [he] said, "Just document the program." So there was a community center program, there was a voter registration program, there was a medical program, and so I just played it by ear for a few days, just to see what the programs were. I didn't do a lot of photographing, and then there was a 4th of July picnic that was held by Mr. Vernon Dahmer, and all of the people from that district in Mississippi were at this picnic. I really started photographing then. Generally what I did was just try to spend some time in each of the programs that were going on that summer. And those things would be interrupted by a beating here, or whatever there. On a few occasions, Sandy would ask if I would photograph something specifically, and then other volunteers would come and spend their vacation time or just a weekend helping out in Mississippi, like the *Cleveland Plain Dealer*, a newspaper in Cleveland, wanted photographs of a rabbi who came [as a volunteer]. So I took pictures of him. I did a lot of different things—I did voter registration—and I just tried to cover as much of the programs as I could. I was able to photograph the children [extensively], but the people, I couldn't photograph for security reasons . . . Nobody was supposed to know where we lived in the [local] houses.

I mean, I couldn't photograph the family where I lived. I did [eventually] but their faces were turned. But the thing is that if [white] people had gotten a hold of my film, the [black] people who lived there could have lost their jobs and been in other serious trouble, if it was known that they were involved with us. Of course, the FBI knew and if the FBI knew then everybody knew [laughs], including the local police and the Klan. But those are the people that I couldn't photograph, and it's always been a sad thing for me, because those people put their lives on the line and this is what the movement was all about, so far as I was concerned, and to a great extent you never see these people, you never see them.

Just one example. I was coming home one night, and it was a little later than I normally would. And we tried to avoid integrated cars, but it was late and I don't know where Doug was and as I lived quite a distance from the office, I went in a car with white volunteers 'cause they lived in the area. We were getting near the street where I lived, which was Klondike Street, and somebody said there was possibly a car following us. So, as I said, we didn't want people to know where we lived, for the safety of the people we lived with, so we circled the block. It's not quite a block, but anyhow we circled the area where I lived. We just wanted to see if the car was following, and it was, and so we went around one more time, with the car behind us. But it was far enough [back] that when we turned the corner I could jump out, the car still moving slowly, and because there was no dome light they didn't know the door was open. So I jumped out and ran through the back yard of the house where I stayed. I wanted to get into the house and get to the front to see what was gonna happen, or to see if I could help in any kind of way if something was gonna happen.

The Wilsons always kept the doors open for me. It was dark and the family was asleep, and I made my way to the front of the house where there was a big window—not a huge window, but the biggest window in the living room where I used to look out behind the curtains. As I made my way to the living room, 'cause I wanted to get to that window to see what was going to happen, I saw a silhouette of Mr. Wilson. He had his left hand, I remember, on the screen door, and he was opening it partially. He was going out, and down in his right hand was a shotgun. He was going outside, and I said, he must have heard me, but I said, "Mr. Wilson?" and he said fairly loudly, "Herbert, are they bothering you?" I said, "No, Mr. Wilson, nobody's bothering me. Please don't go outside." So he just shut the door.

Anyhow, nothing happened that night. As a matter of fact, I never really found out what happened, and that sounds so very damn strange, but it was just constant. I mean, it seems like normally you would want to go up to the guys and say, "What happened?" I mean, I saw the car pass and I saw a car following, but the car that the volunteers were in just kept on going. So it just seemed like the next day you would say, "What the hell happened?" Or "Thank God, you're alive!" But something else happened the next day [laughs]. It was always going on, it was always something happening. But my main point, I guess, is that for years after Mississippi, I would have nightmares about Mr. Wilson walking out on that front there, and God knows what would the hell happen. And this man's family is there, all that he loved, and he's going out there to protect *me*, you know. And so that's just one small, small, small incident of people who would put their lives on the line for you, I mean, because you were trying to help them. And those are the people I really would have loved to photograph.

Notes

1. In April 1960, at the age of twenty-four, Marion Barry became the Student Nonviolent Coordinating Committee's (SNCC) first chairman. He resigned the position in the fall of 1960 but remained deeply involved in SNCC's Mississippi campaign. He helped organize the Mississippi Freedom Democratic Party in the summer of 1964.

2. Created in 1962 by SNCC, CORE (Congress of Racial Equality), and the NAACP, COFO, or the Council of Federated Organizations, was the umbrella organization that unified all the organizations carrying out civil rights programs in Mississippi. COFO also functioned to transfer funds from outside agencies to organizations working in the state.

Maria Varela

Maria Varela was born in Pennsylvania and grew up in the upper Midwest and the Northeast with a rigorous Catholic education. She attended Saint Louis High School in Chicago and then went to Alverno College in Milwaukee, where she became student body president. Throughout her formal education, Varela was involved with the Young Christian Students (YCS) program, which she described as a vigorous social inquiry method that guided Catholic students to bring the church's core spiritual values more meaningfully into daily life.

After graduating from Alverno College in 1961, Valera accepted a two-year position with the national YCS organization and began traveling around the country to assist YCS college chapters and to encourage students to support the expanding Civil Rights Movement. In 1962 Tom Hayden and Al Haber invited her to attend the Port Huron conference as a YCS representative and to participate in shaping what would become the founding document of the Students for a Democratic Society.

In 1963 Varela went south in response to a call to join the Civil Rights Movement. For the next four years, she worked for the Student Nonviolent Coordinating Committee, mainly in the states of Alabama and Mississippi. She initially undertook a literacy project in Selma to promote voter registration. Later, in Mississippi, she turned to photography to illustrate literacy material because she wanted to show "local people taking leadership roles in their own communities." Eventually, Varela edited and/or authored several photo-based publications and filmstrips ranging from voter education training manuals to organizing cooperatives. While with SNCC, she also shot on assignment for the Black Star Photo Agency and the Delta Ministry.

In 1968 Varela was invited to northern New Mexico to start agricultural cooperatives and community health clinics. In 1990 she was awarded a MacArthur Fellowship for her work of organizing Mexican American and Native American weavers and sheep growers to preserve their pastoral cultures and economies. She currently lives in New Mexico and works as a visiting professor at Colorado College in Colorado Springs.

I learned [of SNCC at a National Student Association conference] by listening intently to the African Americans talking about their experiences [during the Freedom Rides] and what the [new] law was—the interstate commerce law—which stated that segregation in interstate terminals was illegal. They had to make that kind of an appeal [to get NSA endorsement for the movement]. And if I remember what was going on, the debate over endorsement just about split NSA open. But people like Connie Curry, who was part of NSA, and Casey Hayden, who was working for the YWCA, were mobilizing [support for SNCC] and a lot of white students were there who were allies of the movement or were advocating for resolutions to come out of the National Student Association.

I supported SNCC because when they told their story it was eminent injustice. It was the kind of thing that if I'd go home and tell my mom about it, she'd say, "Yeah, that's not fair." So because I was raised with a sense of justice and because I came through YCS where we were constantly [working] on issues of injustice and inequity, [I thought] certainly these folks were putting in action Christian values. And what was so interesting to me, they weren't Catholic [laughs]. Here's the Catholic Church saying, it is *the* church, right, it is *the* Christian church, and here are people acting out the gospel in ways that Catholics were not. So that was the appeal to me of SNCC.

Then Casey [Hayden] sent me a letter and asked me to come and work with her. She was staffing the Atlanta [SNCC] office, and I didn't want to go. It was absolutely *not* in my mind to go south. And had she not sent me the letter, I probably would have finished my YCS two years, or maybe I would have gone to [graduate] school, but I wouldn't have gone if somebody hadn't invited me. And that's an organizing principle. Most people won't come to the work unless you get to know them and ask them. It's all about developing relationships, which is what Ella [Baker] taught us.

There wasn't much discussion about voter registration at that point. My sense of the movement came through the students [who were] talking about the bus rides down, the burning of the bus, the sit-ins. And I was awestruck by their courage. I thought, I would never have the courage to do that. You'd never catch me on a bus. I mean, there were people who went down because that really turned their crank. I wasn't one of those people. But I felt honored that Casey asked me, 'cause I really looked up to her as a person—her intellect was incredible. I never met a woman that was so clear about these issues, without being so ideological I couldn't follow her discussions of them. She was a southern woman, unlike me, but she was [also] a woman raised to get married and have a family. And [she] got her activism through the YWCA; so we had that kinda similar thing, about coming up through a progressive, Christian organization. Then here I was going campus-to-campus [through YCS], exhorting students to support the Civil Rights Movement, and that was to me kind of strange that I would refuse the call, but I didn't want to go. I mean, even though I was reassured I'd be in the [Atlanta SNCC] office, I was going to be in a very segregated place, working for an African American organization, and certainly they would be targets.

I probably discussed it with Bill Good, who was the head of our Young Christian Students group. I don't remember those conversations. I didn't talk it over with my parents 'cause I was pretty sure they wouldn't want me to go. They knew I had this graduate fellowship lined up at Marquette, and the idea of going to graduate school was a big deal. So I didn't talk it over with them until I decided to go, and then they weren't happy about it, but they couldn't stop me. I mean, they could have tried; we had discussions, but I'm amazed at how they let me do that. They must have been scared to death. It's like if my daughter would tell me [today] that she was gonna go work with Comandante Marcos, I would be so freaked out I would be doing everything [chuckles] [to stop her]. But in the end, I guess I'd know that it was her decision. I learned that from my parents.

I went down in the summer—actually, I think it was May, because when Connie Curry and Paul Potter, who was part of SDS but then worked for NSA too, heard I agreed to come, they asked me if I would come down in May. They wanted me to work on this summer school for young black activists that NSA put together with cooperation of SNCC around teaching nonviolence and black history, because kids were just willy-nilly walking into drugstores, soda fountains, and Tastee-Freezes, demanding integration. These were thirteen-, fourteen-, fifteen-, sixteen-year-olds, emulating the college kids. And they had no training; they had no discipline. The college kids had been through courses in how to be nonviolent, how to protect yourself. Well, these kids just decided to do it. It was just this thing sweeping the South.

So they pulled in some of the kids, I think they had twenty-three of them, and they asked me to be a staff person. I didn't deliver any of the content of the summer. But we brought in some incredible people like Robert Coles, who came down because he was very concerned about how this was psychologically impacting these kids. I can't remember who else we brought down, but Frank Smith came in from Selma, 'cause SNCC field workers would come in and give presentations to the kids about the work. So I met Frank and he was very interested when he heard I was in the Young Christian Students because he wanted Father Oulette in Selma to be supported because he was the only minister who was willing to let the church be used for voter registration training. The black ministers were too afraid, 'cause [Sheriff] Jim Clark was such a terrorist. And Father Oulette, a French Canadian who himself understood discrimination, was very supportive. And they wanted to keep him as a sort of anchor in Selma, so they just asked me to go. I said, "What will I do?" They said, "Well, Father Oulette wants some more voter registration things to happen, and people can't read, so you could do a literacy project."

When you look back at this time, how would you describe yourself?
What I'm told, especially by people I knew in SDS and in SNCC, was that I never said "boo" at any meeting.

They said, "We'd see you at the far end of the room with those big eyes of yours." I was a sponge. I was just taking all this in. It really intellectually stimulated and spiritually reinforced me. I mean, I was meeting brilliant people, learning things I never learned in college, and I think I was addicted to this. And through relationships they led me into these situations, and I was absorbing everything. I also felt called to be of service where I could have my strength. My strength was not to go up in front and develop protest strategy. My strength was to support. I was raised in that paradigm, and so I was very comfortable as support staff to anything that was going on. And all of these things asked me to be support staff, whether it was Casey in the SNCC office, Paul for the summer program, or Frank saying, "Go in there and support Oulette."

So they had me fly to Selma, and Father Oulette picked me up. And Worth [Long] or whoever was in the SNCC office, which was downtown—St. Edmund's was a little north of town—came over and we had a discussion about what my work would be and what Father and SNCC people thought would be helpful. And they drilled into me that "you're undercover," because this is 1963. This was before the Summer Project. They were concerned about my safety but also the safety of SNCC staff because of how repressive the sheriff, Jim Clark, was. So I was told: "You can't go to the SNCC office. You're to act as though you are a missionary out of St. Edmund's Parish, which means you *can* go to black people's homes because missionaries do that. And if you're teaching reading, you should be safe and so should the person you're teaching reading to be safe."

There was a sense, if we just had some literacy work they [people] could read the new literacy test, which was wrong. I mean, [for] a beginning reader [it] would be very difficult, when I looked at those questions. I mean, some things, yes, but some of the test was designed to be out of the reach of people who were barely literate. But the ultimate strategy was people weren't going to vote because they couldn't read. So let's improve [the] literacy skills people had and help [other] people learn to read so they'd all have the courage to register to vote—knowing that teachers who could read perfectly well were flunking that test anyway. But then you could develop a class-action suit and you could show black people want to vote, 'cause what was being said in the halls of Congress as well as across the South was: "These people don't want to vote!"

Rennie Davis and Paul Potter—my SDS friends—helped a lot. They taught me proposal writing. SNCC was gonna support me; I was on staff, but SNCC didn't say, "You have to raise the money." It was Paul and Rennie's idea. "You can raise money to do this literacy work, so you're not just in there on your own." And it was clear to me that the only way I could do this in Selma would be to have an African American student crew come in, in the summer [of 1964]. It was a no-brainer. I was never even gonna think about bringing in anybody who wasn't black to work in Selma. So I developed a pilot program with Worth Long and Father Oulette and my SDS friends to bring students down and we'd test literacy materials, because when I was looking at all this adult literacy material [we had], [I could see] it was not appropriate. It was just all white families doing things, and it didn't make any sense to use it.

So we set on this *very* ambitious [research] project, since I knew *nothing* about teaching reading or literacy, to find [or create] material. And I went to Bank Street School in New York, which had done some adult literacy work and did UN materials. And then I'd go into St. Edmund's every day and go through it—[and] I just had bunches of literacy kind of stuff, and was grappling with how do you develop these materials. Then Father Oulette suggested that I actually start teaching reading to Mrs. Caffey, who was one of his parishioners. And that's where I learned that when somebody is both intrigued and intimidated by your presence in their house, it's difficult for them to learn. I mean, I decided to use the Bible as a way to start teaching reading because people knew it, and I figured if they could go between what they knew orally and the written page, there would be a connection. But I never knew from her if she was reading or whether she had it

memorized so incredibly that she would [chuckles] act like she was reading.

But she was a great lady. And we went fishing [chuckles]. I had a car, and Father Oulette had sent me, and that meant she had the right to say to me, "Would you like to go fishing?" She had to be in her late seventies, so she wasn't that far away from slavery. And when we'd go fishing, she'd insist on sitting in the back seat, so we were safe. I [think I] really got more out of our transactions than she did, because she opened the door for me to understand how completely people had been made to feel they were inferior and had their place. And from that I could use my intuition to understand that learning to read could mean more than taking a voter registration test. So I realized that we're just gonna have to teach reading in a way that would build people's self-esteem. I would never use that word, because it wasn't used in education classes yet, but some pride, you know. So that's how I got into creating literacy material that could show people's accomplishments, not in the words of some Ph.D., but in their own words. And this is what I wanted the literacy stuff to look like.

The problem with the project was that it wasn't gonna happen in a summer. I was unrealistic about that. But [it was] probably lucky for me the summer [project] did blow up, because then it let me continue to learn more and develop relationships with people working in Mississippi, because it was that staff that would ask me eventually to do these kinds of materials.

Note: SNCC's Selma literacy project blew up because the four students who came down for the summer were exposed as civil rights workers. It happened unexpectedly. On July 3, 1964, the day after the passage of the 1964 Civil Rights Act outlawing segregation in public accommodation, the students wanted to celebrate and went to a local Thirsty Boy ice cream parlor, expecting to be served. Instead, they were arrested, and the project was suddenly "over." "The understanding in a segregated southern town or under apartheid," said Varela, "is that when you cross a [racial] line, you cross the line. So now you're no longer

a literacy worker; you're a rabble-rouser, you're a commu-
nist. You are followed all over town wherever you go. You're
arrested on nothing. You just become harassment bait."
After getting bailed out of jail, the four students spent the
summer as support staff at the local SNCC office, with
one student being invited to join the SNCC staff. Varela
remained undercover for a short time longer and then
relocated to Tougaloo, Mississippi.

In Mississippi I started getting requests to create materials that would support organizers. These were from white volunteers who stayed [after the summer]. I must have run across them when I visited Casey [Hayden] and I'd talk about literacy work and how I was trying to create materials out of people's own stories. So the idea must have come about, well, we could really use X, and I probably said, "I have some money, I can do that." Generally I pestered [SNCC photographer] Bobby Fletcher: "Come with me up to so-and-so. You can take pictures." Finally, he said to me, "Why don't you just take 'em yourself?" I said, "'Cause I don't know how. I don't have a camera." That's when he told me that Matt Herron was supporting the Southern Documentary Project, and if anybody in SNCC wanted to learn photography, they could go to New Orleans and study with him.[1]

I decided to do that 'cause I had money to do materials, and I didn't have any good photographs. And by then I knew you not only had to use the words of [local] people about how they did something, you had to also use pictures showing them taking leadership roles in their own communities. So I did this wonderful week with Matt. I mean, it was incredible being there. Matt had a darkroom, and he got us film and he let us borrow cameras. I think there was at least one other person [with me]—Matt would know who it was. And he trained us to shoot and to print. The greatest thing was he only let us use wide-angle and telephoto [lenses], and now I can't shoot unless I have a wide-angle or a telephoto. It was a wonderful experience.

So then I went back. I took the camera, and I might have gone straight to Batesville, because you can see

some of those shots are pretty shaky. But I didn't see myself becoming a SNCC photographer in the beginning. I was just a person creating things to support organizers. In the Batesville project, these guys were small tenant farmers, growing okra, and they had to rely on a white buyer to sell their crop and they weren't getting a good price. They felt if they could somehow sell together through a co-op they could get a better price. So I brought a tape recorder up, sat Mr. Miles [one of the farmers] down, and told him to take me through what they were doing. Then he helped me set up some shots, [and] we [eventually] created *Something of our Own*, the books on the West Batesville Farmers Cooperative. And then in Holmes County, Mississippi—we did a manual for setting up a political organization. The organizers there did the text, they did the comic book drawings, and then I took the pictures [and] laid it out.

And there was this wonderful African American guy in Jackson who was a printer and who had been in the NAACP since God started the world. He was a veteran, one of those old-timey guys that supported the movement. But education was his bag. Anyway, to make a living he had a printing business, and he would print SNCC flyers. So SNCC people in Jackson said, "Go see Mr. Kirksey." And we developed a great friendship. I brought him business and he taught me how to do layout. He did all my stuff. He was a great mentor, and I *loved* printing books. I loved seeing a project go from beginning [to end]. In the chaos of the movement, the fact that you could [see something go] from beginning to end—create something, you know—kept you from going crazy [laughs].

Matt, I think, criticized my work. He felt it was utilitarian. But I never considered myself an artist. He never told me I was when he trained me. I had a job to do, and I couldn't afford the luxury of being an artist. Had I been a trust fund baby I would have gone that direction, because then it wouldn't have been a problem buying film and just shooting your head off and hating everything and starting all over. But there was a reason I was shooting in the first place, although

I [occasionally] grabbed other shots, just certain things that would catch my eye as well. And basically the theory behind my shooting was: these are strong, beautiful people that are not seen in this country. They are not paid attention to. They are not icon material, you know, but here they are.

And SNCC believed—and we acted on the beliefs and developed organizing [material and] techniques around the belief—that ordinary people can and should speak for themselves and should represent themselves. Therefore, the elite should not be speaking for the so-called downtrodden. They speak for themselves with much more truth, facts, and realism than any interpreter could interpret who they are and what they're going through. That's what we believed. And we were scrupulous in trying to act on that belief in the way we operated. So this infused my photography and the way I developed materials. It infused the organizing methods of the people in the field. It infused both our small discussions, as we hung together over food and beer or whatever, and our staff meetings. There wasn't really anybody else—and I don't wanna sell everybody short—but nobody was doing what our staff was doing in terms of exposing themselves to extreme danger, every day, every day, every day, for years, some of them. And just based on the faith that [it helped] the people they were working for. You know, what keeps you going in this kind of work is you see people change. It's like a teacher, when you see a student and you teach to their assets instead of their deficits, they change. They really change in good ways, and we would see that in communities. We would work with people's assets, their strengths, and not their deficits, and therefore they took hold. So that was basically a mantra for SNCC. That's what kept us going.

Note

1. Matt Herron and his wife, Jeannine, and their two young children settled in Mississippi in 1963 to participate in the movement. They were one of the very few families to move south to join the Southern Freedom struggle. In the fall of 1964, they opted to relocate to New Orleans in part because they had to enroll their two young children in school and didn't want them attending schools in Mississippi, and in part because Herron hoped he could find the resources to sustain the Southern Documentary Project (SDP). Herron envisioned, funded, and directed SDP through the summer of 1964 (please see his interview for additional details), and, upon moving to New Orleans, he built an extensive darkroom in his backyard with the expectation that he would locate additional financial resources to continue the work of photodocumenting the South in the civil rights era. Unfortunately, these resources never materialized. Movement people like Maria Varela, Bob Fletcher, and others, however, heard of Herron's effort to sustain SDP and began to come through New Orleans to ask for support for their efforts to photograph the movement. And though Herron never formally "taught" any of them, he did, he explained, spend considerable time with them, helping them develop darkroom skills, discussing photography, looking at their pictures, offering criticism, and giving informal assignments as a way of dealing with the weak spots in their skills. "Years later at the time of the first Smithsonian civil rights exhibition [in 1981]," Herron said, "I was amazed to learn that a lot of [these] people identified me as their 'teacher.' I guess I probably was."

George "Elfie" Ballis (1925–2010)

George "Elfie" Ballis died on September 24, 2010, in his home in Tollhouse, California, from complications caused by pancreatic cancer.

The firstborn child of Greek and German immigrants, he was raised in the small town of Faribault, Minnesota. After graduating high school in 1943, he rejected a football scholarship to the University of Minnesota and joined the Marine Corps. In boot camp, he tested high for math and science, was sent to radar school, and then was assigned to repair torpedo bombers in the South Pacific. At the war's end, he returned to Minnesota, earned a degree in journalism, and underwent a shift in consciousness that would essentially determine the course of his life. "The Marines made a man out of me," he said. "But it wasn't their man."

In 1951 Ballis was employed as an editor for a string of local Chicago papers when he discovered his "love" of photography. Two years later, he answered an ad and became the editor of the Valley Labor Citizen, *an AFL-CIO newspaper in Fresno. One of his first projects was a series of picture essays on the dignity of farm labor. Equipping himself with a cheap camera, Ballis transformed himself from a reporter with a camera to a photographer with an eye for significant detail. Over the next two decades, he immersed himself in what he described as the two central political issues facing California, farm labor and water. In the process, he amassed more than thirty thousand images on farm labor, the largest body of work by any photographer covering the subject.*

In 1963 Ballis responded to a call for help from the Student Nonviolent Coordinating Committee (SNCC) and drove a donated car packed with office equipment to Greenwood, Mississippi. He stayed in Greenwood for a month, taking photos and learning about SNCC's organizing methods. In 1964, at the suggestion of Dorothea Lange, he was selected to participate in the summer-long Southern Documentary Project, an ambitious undertaking created by photographer Matt Herron to document the South in the midst of the civil rights revolution.

After the project, Ballis returned to Fresno and steadily expanded his social justice activities to include training community organizers, advocating for Native American tribes, and battling the U.S. Bureau of Reclamation to enforce the 1902 law limiting California landowners to owning 160 acres of irrigated land. The decade-long court battle also involved Ballis with the emerging movements for solar energy and organic food production. Reflecting on his lifelong activism in 2004, Ballis said what kept him from burning out was dropping his "warrior's" approach and becoming a "dancer."

"In my younger days, in the beginning of time [laughs], after the Marine Corps, I viewed myself as a warrior, and I said, 'In order to be effective, I've gotta maintain my anger so I have the energy to do this.' And then, and this was not an intellectual process, I started dancing with it. By the 1960s, I'm no longer George. I'm pretty much Elfie. I'm feeling like I don't want to destroy capitalism. What I want to do, if I had my way with the world, is to cure those people who are in charge of their obsession with greed and control."

I was born on August 12, 1925, in my grandmother's living room in Kaukauna, Wisconsin, and the first thing I remember on coming into this reality was my chubby German auntie saying, "Isn't he cute?" And, of course, I was. I don't remember much after that, except I remember the Mayo Clinic a little bit. I'm ten and I'm going in for this serious operation. They're laying me on a table and this nurse comes over, and they're gonna put me away. She starts putting this thing on my mouth and she said, "You don't have to be afraid of us." I looked up into her eyes and said, "I'm not afraid of you guys." The next memory I have of the Mayo Clinic is waking up from the second—I had two complicated operations on my urinary tract. I'm groggy in bed, and these guys in white coats are standing a little ways away from the bed, having this conversation. They think I'm still out of it, and what they're saying in effect is, "This kid's not long for this world."

• • •

I grew up in Faribault, Minnesota. It's about fifty-five miles south of Minneapolis, a little town, maybe thirteen thousand [people]. My father was a Greek immigrant, and there were several Greek families in Faribault. Most of them were in the restaurant

business, but my father and his brother were in a dry cleaning and shoe repair business. We were, in effect, the niggers of Faribault. I remember in third grade a kid called me a "greasy Greek." I started to beat the shit out of him, and a teacher came up, tried to pull us apart, and I turned around and slugged him. The thing I remember about that now is my mother wasn't too angry. I was thinking, "Whoa, God, I'm gonna really get it!" She wasn't too angry. She was, in effect, giving me license to stand up for my rights and my dignity. She is the key to who I really am. Not only did I come out of her womb, but I came out of her soul. I mean, she gave me license to speak out and stand up. I remember [chuckles] her remark about the Civil Rights Movement was, "What the hell took them so long?"

The other thing my mother did was when I came off this Mayo Clinic thing and all these operations and the tube up your penis and all that kind of stuff, I was a very frail eleven-year-old, bed-wetting kid. Well, by the time I got thirteen, I was still just a skinny little kid, and it came time in my town for the boys to play football. My father said, "No, he's too weak!" My mother said, "He's gonna play football." She *made* me play football. And for the first couple years, I got the shit kicked out of me, because I was small. But by the time I was a junior, I'd beefed up to about 185 pounds, and I was the quarterback. I made up plays on the field, I was the captain of the football team, and I made all-state and got a football scholarship.

But the interesting thing about my parents is they never owned a car. My father's business was less than a block away [from our home], and both my mother and father worked in that business. They never went on vacation. They never went anyplace. I never went anywhere until I got that football scholarship to the University of Minnesota. Then my parents put me on a bus, and I went to Minneapolis by myself, went to see the coach. They got me a room at the firehouse and free rent and all that. And so I left the university [campus], went downtown to get a bus, and I was standing on a street corner, and all of a sudden I said [to myself], I'm not gonna play football. I'm gonna join the Marine Corps. My mother's only complaint was, "I just bought him new underwear so he could go to the university!" [Laughs.] And that was the second most important decision of my life, because I learned in the Marine Corps what I *never* could learn in the university or out of any book or from any professor—real-life, gut, bloody shit.

I joined in 1943, and the war was on. And they sent me to boot camp in San Diego. I had been to Minneapolis three times in my life, and now I'd go all the way across the country. I thought it was a gas. I went to boot camp in San Diego. While I'm in boot camp, they gave us aptitude tests, right. So I scored high in math and science, 'cause I'm a natural mathematician. Most of the guys in my platoon went to Camp Pendleton to infantry. I went to radar tech school, first in Chicago and then in Corpus Christi. And I'm alive this day because of that twist of fate. Because about half the guys, most of them eighteen, nineteen, twenty years old [like me], were dead within six months, because they were taking these goddamn Pacific islands one by one in '43, '44. I was devastated when I found out about it after I got out of the Marine Corps, because taking those islands was total propaganda, total photo ops. They had nothing whatsoever to do with military strategy, because in December of 1942, the U.S. Navy almost destroyed the Japanese navy at the Battle of Midway, so the U.S. controlled the Pacific. But they wanted to keep the war fever up, so they stormed the beaches with tough eighteen-year-old cherries being heroic and getting their asses shot off. I had other experiences in the Marine Corps, which led me to believe I can't trust authority, period. But *that* realization didn't come while I was in the corps; it came after [I left].

In 1946 I was discharged and started doing construction jobs in Minneapolis. Then I decided to go to the University [of Minnesota], because I've got the G.I. bill. I'll get ninety bucks a month, plus all the books, right. Besides, I knew I could do this engineering bullshit. Anyway, I go to engineering school and the first quarter I get As in everything, high math, physics,

chemistry, the full catastrophe. I can do it like nothing. It's like a cakewalk. So towards the end of the quarter, the flip comes. I look at my grades, I said, God, I have the ability to become a great engineer, maybe even be famous, but I wouldn't have any control over what I did. The same bastards who killed my buddies for photo ops would control it. So I jumped out of the engineering school and went to liberal arts. And I think the main thing in my recollection now is that it was like that previous decision to join the Marine Corps. It was an epiphany. Is that what they call it? I switched during Christmas break, and I later got a degree with a double major in political science and journalism.

Then Marti [my first wife] and I moved to Chicago where I became a police reporter for the city news bureau, and that's where I learned firsthand about police brutality. I identified this one so-called gangster who was shot by a cop, and it turned out he was sitting in a car and the cop walked up to the window and shot him in the head. Then I got a job as assistant editor of a string of Chicago weeklies run by a Republican councilman. My job was to edit the paper and lay out the pages. People would bring in photographs, and they were so bad. You can imagine, Grandma up against the wall kind of thing, out of focus. I said, "Shit, I could do better than that." So I bought a camera and a book and started shooting pictures. And the first roll of pictures—I wish I'd have saved them!—was in an ethnic market in West Chicago. I had this 35mm, and I'd just get next to these people and start shooting. And it was love at first click. I said, Wow, this is great! Nobody pays attention to what these people are doing, and I can pay attention to it. So that's where it all started. And the only photographic course I've ever taken is the seminar with Dorothea Lange.[1]

In January '53, I see this ad for editor of the AFL-CIO weekly newspaper owned by the Central Labor Council and the Building Trades Council. I apply for the job. I do a month trial and the guy hires me, and we move to Fresno. So this is perfect, right. I started photographing farm workers. I started working on the water issue. Because when I got to Fresno, in a short while I perceived that the two main political problems in California are farm labor and water, and I started working on both of them. And what I did, I made a practice of calling the local unions every week before I wrote the paper and saying, "What's going on?" And they'd say, "Nah, nothing's happening," or they'd give me a story, and I'd photograph picket lines or whatever and write it up.

At the same time, I started walking out to labor camps and talking to people and photographing them. Most of the time it was okay. Once in a while a farmer would chew my ass out and throw me out. But with the farm workers it didn't come clean so easily. I weigh 175 pounds at the time, right. I'm crew cut. I'm a blue-eyed devil. I look like an all-American boy, and so I had to go out and save these people. I didn't even know Dorothea [Lange] existed when I started in '54, '55. So I'm gonna go out and expose the terrible conditions these people live under, and then the society will change it—[that's] my mindset. It changed very quickly, because I went out looking like this [gestures downward with his hand], and then, very shortly, I am looking like this [gesturing straight across]. And they *felt* that difference. So I realized my job was not to expose these conditions, my job was to celebrate the strength and power of these people, and amplify it with my camera. And that became my vision of what I was doing.

What brought you down from the pedestal?
Well, it's one thing to talk about people in a condition; it's another thing to look somebody in the eye. When I did that, I saw me, I saw we. I didn't see them any more, I saw us. So I'm not working on *their* issues, I'm working on *our* issues. We're all in this together—whether it's farm labor conditions or civil rights or gay marriages or the conditions of the steelworkers, it's us. So that makes it easy for me to work on gay marriages one day and union organizers the next day, because I see us. I don't see them gays or them hospital workers, I see us. I literally see us. It's not like this is an intel-

lectual process. I'm with them, I am them; we're us, so to speak.

Like when I went to Mississippi the first time in '63, I took a car down there and a bunch of office supplies. A SNCC worker had come to Fresno and did a little speaking to us. "You can help us out by sending us materials." I said, "Fine." I had a wife and two kids at that time, and people around Fresno are saying, "Why the hell are you doing this? Why the hell are you going to Mississippi? That's *their* problem!" I'd say, "It's not their problem, it's *our* problem, because if they're deprived, we're deprived. And this is '63. They had quite a discussion around town among the so-called white progressives about my going to Mississippi, because by then I'm no longer a kid. They're saying, "Well, if you were a college kid, nineteen or twenty years old, but you're what, [almost] forty years old now." I said, "Well, I've gotta do it." That's what I always do. And that's why Maia [my second wife] and I, we've stuck together. It's not even appropriate to call it walking the talk, it seems to me. It's living your life.

Do the farm worker photos you later took reflect that change in perspective?
I think the pictures look different. I wish I had those pictures of Chicago, that first roll of film I took. It was there but I didn't recognize it. I was just *doing* it. And that's easy when you've not been schooled, perfect for me anyway. You don't go, "Well, this is the exposure and this is how composition looks, and you've gotta have it one-third this way," or any of that bullshit, you just do it. As I remember it now, it was there but I didn't know what it was. And when I first came here, I was following the white middle-class radical view: we're gonna save all those people, because that's one of the problems the farm workers' movement had. I had a lot of arguments with people down at Delano about doing the noble savage kind of thing, which is bullshit. I said, "They're *us!* They're just the same as us. Some are drunks, some are assholes, some are beautiful people, but they're us!" That's the important consid-

eration. If you go down there [thinking], I'm gonna save these people, that's crap. What we want to do is empower each other. If people become empowered, then they become responsible.

I like to say I take photographs or films of *extra*-ordinary people who are trying to make a change in their lives and in the world. And the hope is that they will look at it and see themselves as somebody in power and other people will look at it and say, "Oh, Joe did that. I could do that." That's the organizing part of it. Because I want to encourage people to grab it, and the people who are grabbing it I like to show them, and I don't like to show the famous people particularly. I concentrate on showing the ordinary folk, like the woman on the cross outside her shack who looks like somebody, although she's poor.[2] Or like the other people on the street who look like anybody. It's all about improving our joint condition, our relationships, improving God even, 'cause we're part of God. I don't see God out there. I don't see Allah, I don't see Moses, I don't see Jesus, I see us.

I remember in 1963 when I went to Greenwood, Mississippi, I left the car and hung out for three weeks and then rode a bus back. Hardly got any sleep at all [laughs]. I slept almost all the way back to California. That's one thing I remember, and I got to know Bob Moses, an incredible guy. I remember the SNCC meetings that would go on and on and on. But it wasn't like committee meetings. He was trying to reach consensus and understanding, and it was great to be a part of that process and photograph it. I learned a lot from Bob. They were doing a voter registration drive, so I did a lot of photographing around the clerk's office and the picket lines and people going in and out of the courthouse. I met some powerful people at the meetings like Fannie Lou Hamer and some of the older people who were really sticking their necks out. That was amazing to see that courage and to be part of it and to try to amplify it.

In the summer of '64, I went back. At that point, I got into Jackson on a bus and got a car, and I went to the SNCC office. They said, "We want you to go to [James] Chaney's funeral in Philadelphia," so I drove out to Philadelphia. I had on this old, loose-fitting suit and a tie, [with] my usual crew cut, and I walked into this hall where they're having a memorial service. People are looking. None of them know me, right. Who the hell is this guy? I noticed one guy went to the phone and called the headquarters of SNCC in Jackson. I didn't hear him, but I saw him on the phone and then I noticed that he hung up and came back and said, "It's all right. The gentleman that just entered is one of us" [laughs].

Note

1. Ballis took a photography seminar from Dorothea Lange in Fresno in 1958.

2. Ballis refers to a photo he made in a migrant camp in Tulare County, California, in 1968. In the photo, a Latino woman in her twenties, wearing jeans and a work shirt, leans against a cross-shaped wood post that serves as the end of a clothes line. She's clearly "on the cross." But just as clearly, her cross—her life as a migrant worker—doesn't daunt her. She slouches with subtle defiance, left hand on hip, cigarette in right hand, and looks into the distance.

Bob Fitch

Bob Fitch was a student at the Pacific School of Religion in the mid-1960s when he began his career as an activist photographer. Trained to be a Protestant minister and expected to take a pulpit, he says, "Photojournalism seduced me. It is a compelling combination of visual aesthetics, potent communication, and storytelling. It is a way to support the organizing for social justice that is transforming our lives and future."

Shortly after working for the Glide Foundation in San Francisco, Fitch became a staff photographer for the Southern Christian Leadership Conference (SCLC), led by Rev. Martin Luther King. Traveling throughout Alabama, Mississippi, and Georgia, Fitch documented movement events, including community organizing, violence against African Americans, voter registration, and political campaigns. His images and stories were shipped to national African American publishing outlets that could neither afford nor risk sending reporters to the South. Many of his best images document the courageous contribution made to the Civil Rights Movement by the men, women, and children who organized in the cause of freedom in their local communities.

Fitch returned to California in 1966 and began to document the peace and social justice activities on the West Coast, focusing on Dorothy Day and the Catholic Worker houses of hospitality; the first congressional campaign of California Congressman Ron Dellums; and the organizing efforts of Cesar Chavez and the United Farm Workers Union. The 2002 Cesar Chavez stamp issued by the U.S. Post Office is a rendering of a Fitch photo.

Throughout the 1980s and 1990s Fitch immersed himself in a variety of human services programs. He photographed less, but continued to actively "use any media necessary" to support organizing efforts. After leaving state service, he settled in Santa Cruz, California, where he worked for the Resource Center for Nonviolence (RCNV), a thirty-year-old community-based nonprofit that supports various local and national peace and social justice programs. Fitch currently lives in Watsonville, California, where he continues to work in behalf of organized labor and peace and justice campaigns.

I started meddling with photography in junior high school out of sheer amazement. I mean, you take this piece of paper out of the camera, put it in a little container, add some chemicals and poof, you get a negative. Shine a light through that on some paper, put that piece of paper in some chemicals and poof, this picture appears. Total magic. But I photographed intermittently [until seminary]. I'd pick up a camera, I'd do some work. In college, I photographed for the newspaper. Because there wasn't a photographer, I filled a hole, but not very well. So I kept those skills growing a little bit. Then [in seminary] I read Baldwin's *The Fire Next Time*. I'd gotten into it at about eleven at night. It was a class assignment, and I couldn't put it down. I don't know how much Baldwin you've read, but he's *vivid*. You can feel, smell, taste, and see when you read Baldwin, and *The Fire Next Time* is this amazing prophecy. Baldwin takes off on this theme [based on] living in Harlem and the building anger and frustration of black people. It's a *stunning* book. At the end of the reading, about four in the morning, I had a vision that somehow, someway I would aesthetically be portraying elements in that book.

After this settled down, I was in my chair, thinking, if this is gonna happen, writing is a pain in the ass for me. I can't draw for shit. What's it gonna be? Well, within a week, I bought my first professional level, used camera back, 35mm lens, 100mm lens, and started to photograph. And then civil rights activity in San Francisco came along, [the] Free Speech Movement came along, and I began to photograph here and there. Glide really shaped that. Glide Church was a Methodist church in the inner city of San Francisco that had been set up by the Glide family of California oil wealth to evangelize in the inner city. And they meant old-style evangelism. Well, they got a new bishop and he said, "We're going to start evangelizing in a different way. We're going to assist gangs to pull out of their warfare; we're going to assist the counterculture to stabilize its communes and its newspapers; we're going to assist the gay and the lesbian community to empower themselves in the political sphere; [and] we're going to feed and house and clothe the poor and the homeless in the Tenderloin where we're located."

And they brought in a team of four *very* tough, brilliant organizers, and they started getting interns from my seminary, the Pacific School of Religion, and I was one of the first. I got pulled into the Mission District to work with a church that's in the mission now. And, actually, I fucked up, and they pulled me out. My wife [at the time] ended up having a quasi–love affair with a gang leader, and he and I ended up in a fight one night and he ended up back in prison because he wasn't supposed to use his fists on anybody. I was just a stupid, naïve kid on the street, so they pulled me out. But then they hooked me up with the publishing side, which was publishing books on inner city action issues, and [they] asked me to do some photography for them.

That's where things really started for me in photography. I had no formal training, [so] I began ferociously, and vigorously consuming books about photographers—Cartier-Bresson being a lead mentor philosophically and Dorothea Lange. I took every free course I could. I talked to everybody I could, and I was surprised. I did well. I had a pretty good eye.

By then Don Kuhn [Glide's executive director] saw the photos and saw a way to add illustrations to the books he was working on. I did photography with them for over two years and then after [graduating from] seminary, I wrote to friends at SCLC. I had invited them up as speakers and raised money for them for three years, so I wrote 'em and said, "What would it be like if I came down as a photographer?" I knew that after Selma there would be a big exodus and everybody would go home. And the big chore after Selma would be getting some people elected. So they said, "Oh, that'd be cool. We don't have anybody right now, and nobody stays after they sell a few photos."

Another part of my decision to go south to work for the black Civil Rights Movement was my father, who taught ethics at my seminary. He was a man who received all his information by reading books or journals, and he was a tremendous researcher. He would reread

Socrates, Plato, Herodotus, Hume, and Berkeley every ten years, and he collected all their statements that correlated with Christian teachings. So I made a vow to myself early in my graduate years: I am going to be someone who doesn't read about it, but someone who goes there and experiences it. I want to smell it and feel it and taste it.

So a hunk of my decision to go south was the sense that now I've got all this education, I've got all this academic work, now I'm gonna go and be there.

I piled my cameras in a bag—by then I was out of my first marriage—and I got down there. My primary contact [in Atlanta] was Hosea Williams. He was the field organizer, and I learned [from him] they couldn't send black photographers into the field. They'd get the crap beat out of 'em, or they were killed. The newspapers and magazines—*Ebony, Jet, Philadelphia Courier,* the *Amsterdam News,* all the newspapers across the country that were Afro—couldn't afford to send their own correspondents down there, much less risk it. So Hosea Williams pointed a finger at me and said, "We're gonna send your little white ass into the field. And we want you to be a wire service, and every week, if possible, we want you to send out photos and stories."

So very shortly, every week, with the help of wire service reporters who taught me how to survive in the field, I began turning in stories. If I have any regret it is that I didn't have more journalistic training. I didn't have a keen sense of the cosmic time I was in. But a few people like Flip Schulke, a *Life* photographer finally knocked on my head and said, "Hey, guy, you're in the middle of history. Be more thoughtful about getting pictures." Joe Holloway, a UPI photographer, was another mentor. Joe was a southerner. He never took sides, although he was emotionally very much on the side of integration. He was just clever at getting around and not getting hurt. And he showed me how to be respectful and cool with southerners. He also took me into the UPI labs and showed me how to develop and print in a bathroom, when you're on the road and you're in a motel room. He taught me this

whole kinda behind-the-scenes urgency technology they were using.

So then Hosea or Andy [Young] started giving me assignments. And a routine assignment was a Dr. King Alabama speaking tour, where you'd be lined up for two or three days and eight to twelve churches. The tour would encourage voter registration or support candidates in local communities where candidates would come forward and offer to run for sheriff or justice of the peace or school board. And these were a kick in the ass, because Dr. King and Andy [Young] liked to drive at eighty, ninety miles an hour. So there'd be Dr. King's car, Andy driving and Hosea with them; then would come a couple of staff cars, I might be in one of 'em; then would come the conventional press. So you had this caravan, tearing down these two-lane back roads. Normally the cops would arrest these drivers, but it was Dr. King, who was a global personality by that time, so they didn't stop the caravan. And so for two or three days we just tore across the state, stopping in a little church for a sermon, little food, shaking hands, and photographs.

Another assignment, particularly around the campaign, was they wanted headshots of every candidate running for office. They'd give me names, they'd give me towns, they'd give me a contact in the town, [and this was] all over Alabama, and they'd stick me in a car and send me off. A third type came when something happened in a given town—like Beets Field, Alabama, was having a series of marches to boycott the stores in downtown because they won't hire any blacks. I'd stay for a week, photograph, and get the story out.

And [after a while] I could see that Doc[1] kinda got to like me. He became like an older brother to me. It was a very special relationship, and he was great to be with. He was funny and affable, and he had an intensity that engaged people. So when he was with someone, he was *with* them. It was really powerful to see him during a break in a campaign when people would gather and he'd hold these intimate conversations. Then at night we'd relax and tell stories. We'd be a bunch of people in a room, and they'd tell stories and laugh and holler. I don't know whether you've ever been around physicians. They have kind of an emergency room humor. This was kind of near-death humor.

I carried out these assignments for about a year and a half, and I was very successful. I'd come back on a Wednesday or Thursday or Friday and I developed film, made a bunch of prints. I had a bunch of boxes for the different places where I would send them, write cutlines for the prints, Scotch tape 'em on, and write a little story to go with a print or several prints, stuff it in an envelope and send it off. Sometimes up to a dozen to the major black press across the country, including *Jet* and *Ebony*. Then, I don't know if you remember, but all these Afro newspapers across the country would hit the newsstand on Tuesday. Sometimes they wouldn't arrive [in Atlanta] 'til Wednesday. I'd go down on Wednesday and I'd walk across the newsstand at the drugstore, and there were my photos, complete captions with no editing. So I quickly saw a huge amount of my work published as featured articles. And SCLC was ecstatic.

What impression were you getting of the South in all these travels and activities?

Well, for me, it was like—eyes wide, Bob, you know. The South was a brand-new experience for me. I'd never been there, wasn't acquainted with the culture, either the white or the black culture. And at that time the reason I was sending press releases and photos to major black newspapers was that Afro-American culture was totally isolated and separate from Anglo culture. And black people had their own entertainment, their own newspapers, their own banks, their own pharmacies in most urban communities. So it was like going to another planet, and that's a planet where I had never lived.

So everything I did was new [laughs], *really* new, and the people I was meeting were really new for my life. I remember they once sent me out—I've got a photograph of this—to meet an old, old man who'd

been born in slavery, take his picture, and make a feature article. He had never been out of the thirty-mile radius of his home. I had never met anyone like that. I remember writing an article and sending out the photos with it. I still have the photo, but not the notes. I deeply regret that I wasn't more meticulous about that. I also remember a silly experience that'll give you an idea of some of my middle-class upscale breeding. I went to a minister's house to talk to him and his wife. They were gonna put me up for a half day until I did other photos. I went in the bathroom and I gave a shit, and I looked around. I needed to wipe my ass and there was no toilet paper. I wondered, "How am I gonna wipe my ass?" So I tapped on the door, and said, "Mrs., do you have any toilet paper?" She said, "Wait just a minute." I waited ten minutes—suddenly a roll of toilet paper was handed to me. On the floor was a box of bundled-up newspapers. That's what they used for toilet paper. They literally went to the store and bought me a roll of toilet paper, this *incredible* luxury. I didn't have the brains quite to put that together until a little later. So it was a new world for me.

And they were good people, *really*, really good people. And I remember driving, and being extremely scared. I remember sometimes we'd drive from Selma back to Atlanta, and LeRoy Moton was the young man who was in the car with Viola Liuzzo[2] when she was killed. And it was *incredibly* scary for him to drive that road still. He was in a state of fear, and he'd often get himself drunk to be able to take that drive back to Atlanta. You know, one day I detected he was just so fucking drunk, and I asked one of the guys, "Why does he do that to himself?" He explained the story as I've just shared it with you. And sometimes I would actually weep when I'd be in a church. You know, we were so unsafe and under threat on the street and had to be so careful that to be in a church and the *safety* of that circumstance would overwhelm me as the music would start up, and I'd just break into tears.

The first time I drove back from the South to visit the West, I got into California and I was driving down the highway and a highway patrol car drove up behind me. He pulled up and he passed me, and I broke into weeping and had to pull over and stop the car, because the everyday fear for all of us was just so fucking intense it was not conscious. It had to be denied. And I'm proud to say this in behalf of the black Civil Rights Movement that many people in the North [still] don't understand. They say, "Oh, it was a failure, it didn't raise the salaries of . . ." Well, it failed on many levels, particularly economically. But a person who has never been there will never understand what it's like for a family, for the first time in a hundred years to walk at night with safety down a main street of their own town, be that Eutaw, Alabama, or Atlanta, Georgia—'cause to do that prior to the black Civil Rights Movement meant death or a beating or severe harassment.

[I have a final] story and for me this is critical. I have a set of heroes that has endured a lifetime from this experience. I was in Eutaw, Alabama, and this was the beginning of the voter rights campaigns, and our attorneys and NAACP and ACLU were beginning to purge the rolls of the dead Anglo people [chuckles]. Everything was very tense, but this was a target town for SCLC. Eventually a preacher there became the first black sheriff since Reconstruction in the South. Lee was his last name, [he] could never carry a gun. But I was in town photographing candidates, and I passed a school. Someone had told me it was an all-white school, one of the segregated schools. I'd visited a black school, but I just stopped the car to photograph this school. I stepped on the grass, and suddenly a cop came up, grabbed my ass, threw me in the cop car, took me to jail for four days. They wouldn't let me make a call. But people knew where I was and somehow the word got out, and after four days of eating beans, a lot of cornbread and beans, they brought me downstairs and they said I'd been bailed out.

I said, "Oh, wonderful. Let's see the papers." They put them before me. I had to sign them. And my thoughts were, well, who bailed me out? And Dr.

King's name was not on the bail-out papers. Andrew Young's name was not on the papers, and Hosea Williams's name was not on the papers. The names that were on the papers were three local farmers, who had put up their lifetime heritage—their land—to bail my white ass out of jail. It was a very stark reminder of something I knew was going on but became very sharp as the movement went on, that the black Civil Rights Movement was not the result of Dr. King, or Stokely Carmichael, or CORE or any civil rights organization. The black Civil Rights Movement was a consequence of hundreds and thousands of landed and employed Afro-American families nickel and diming to their own local organizations for the century after Reconstruction. These farmers were part of that, and that's what bailed my white ass out of jail. Even telling you today it tingles. And that's been my role model for the rest of my life. The rest of my life is: Bob, you're in a community. Be attentive to that community. Be attentive to the social justice issues in that community. And support the empowerment of the disenfranchised, wherever you're living. So pretty much after I left SCLC I did various kinds of organizing for the balance of my life and photographed those activities as I went through. And I perceived myself as an organizer who uses a camera to tell the story of my work, which is true today.

Notes

1. "Doc" was a nickname for Dr. Martin Luther King, Jr.

2. Viola Liuzzo, a thirty-nine-year-old mother of five, was killed by the KKK on March 25, 1965. A white activist from Michigan, Liuzzo participated in the Selma to Montgomery march and was driving marchers back to Montgomery when a car with three passengers pulled alongside of her and one of the men shot her in the head. At the time of the shooting, LeRoy Moton, a nineteen-year-old black activist, was sitting in the front passenger seat of the car Liuzzo was driving.

Matt Herron

Matt Herron has been a photojournalist since 1962, and his pictures have appeared in virtually every major picture magazine in the world. Based in Mississippi in the early 1960s, he covered the civil rights struggle for Life, Look, Time, Newsweek, *and the* Saturday Evening Post, *as well as providing pictures for the Student Nonviolent Coordinating Committee (SNCC). In 1964 he founded and directed the Southern Documentary Project, a team of six photographers that attempted to document the process of social change in the South. The project worked closely with SNCC's photographic team and shared their Atlanta darkroom. During that period, Herron also provided basic training for many SNCC staff members interested in utilizing photographs in their organizing activities.*

In the late 1960s, Herron worked with New Orleans District Attorney Jim Garrison in investigating the assassination of President John F. Kennedy. During that period he also founded and administered the Listening Eye Gallery, a New Orleans photographers' cooperative. In 1970, he set sail in a small boat with his wife and two children, bound for the west coast of Africa. The family spent a year and a half crossing the Atlantic and exploring eight West African countries. Their book, The Voyage of Aquarius, *documents that quest. In the 1970s, Herron turned to writing, and produced a series of major articles for the* Smithsonian *and other publications. He also became involved in ecology action, serving as bridge officer, navigator, and photographer on two Greenpeace antiwhaling voyages and a voyage to the ice floes of the St. Lawrence to protest the harp seal hunt. In the late 1980s Herron became involved in labor organizing, serving for twelve years as a director and then as president of the American Society of Media Photographers, the major trade organization that represents photographers who shoot for publication.*

A nationally recognized social documentary photographer, Herron has work in the permanent collections of the George Eastman House, the Schomburg Center for Research in Black Culture, and the Smithsonian Institution. At present, he directs Take Stock, a picture agency that specializes in licensing the work of activist photographers.

[My wife], Jeannine, and I began to talk about joining the movement [in 1963] as a way of working toward nonviolence in the country, which was our creed. That's what we thought might actually make social change. And here was Martin Luther King who had developed the philosophy during the Montgomery bus boycott, and the Freedom Riders had not resisted being beaten, and so this seemed like the way to go. And we were active in the peace movement. Jeannine had joined an early peace group called Women Strike for Peace[1] and [in 1962] had gone to Geneva with Coretta [Scott] King to demonstrate at a disarmament conference.

Then in June 1963, Jeannine got a call from a colleague in Women Strike for Peace from Jackson. She said, "A civil rights leader's been killed here. His name is Medgar Evers. There's going to be a funeral cortege at the end of the week and there aren't many white faces in town. Would you come down?" This coincided with our increasing interest in whether it would be possible for us to move south and join the movement. So Jeannine went down with two goals: one was to march in Medgar Evers's funeral cortege and the other was to find out whether it would be safe for us with two small children [ages three and five] to move to Mississippi and join the movement, 'cause we didn't want to put our kids in danger. She met Ed King, who was a white chaplain at the black college of Tougaloo, just outside Jackson, and the only white Mississippian who had joined the Civil Rights Movement outright (he was number one on the Klan's death list), and she explained what we were thinking. Ed said, "If you move into a white neighborhood in Jackson and you're discreet, you can do it without danger to your children." So that's what we did. We packed our Volkswagen bus and headed south in the summer of 1963.

The first real southern city we hit was Birmingham. We came into Birmingham tired and dirty on a Sunday morning. The church bells were playing Dixie. We looked for a laundromat to wash our clothes. We found one, we were bundling our clothes when I looked at the storefront and saw a sign that said, "White only." We said to each other, "We ain't gonna wash our clothes

here." And being in the Deep South for the first time, pretty scared of the whole thing, convinced us we should go to church and we should find a black church. The closest church to the laundromat was the 16th Street Baptist Church right in the heart of Birmingham, so we went there. The church was very welcoming and in the middle of the service, [our daughter] Melissa had to go pee-pee, and Jeannine took her to the basement to the girls' bathroom and sat her on the potty, and two weeks later the Klan set off a bomb against that side of the building and four little black girls were killed in that same basement. So that was our introduction to the South.

We continued on to Jackson; we stayed with Ed at Tougaloo for a week or so until we were able to rent a house in a mid-to lower-income white neighborhood. And my feeling was: I've been successful making story suggestions [to magazines]. So now I'm south, I'm meeting the SNCC movement people, and Ed was introducing me to everybody and Tougaloo was kind of a center of that, so I thought, I can now make story suggestions that are more profound and truthful and closer to the center of things than I could from Philadelphia. So I should be able to get assignments here. And I very consciously felt myself as wearing three hats. I was a budding photojournalist, that was foremost, and that was how I was gonna support the family. I was also a propagandist for the movement. When movement people wanted pictures I did it and they used them, so that was hat number two. And I thought of propaganda in the good sense of the word, espousing a cause. Third was, I guess, the influence of Dorothea Lange who I had met several times and showed work to and was profoundly influenced by—I wanted to do social documentary work on the way of life that was southern, both black and white, and to try and document this weird culture that we'd thrust ourselves into.

How did Jeannine and you articulate to yourselves what you were doing at this time?
We [felt we] were coming down to put our shoulders

to the wheel of civil rights, with a personal mission to advance the cause of nonviolence within the Civil Rights Movement. The movement was committed to nonviolence as a tactic, not a belief, and we wanted to work with that. We saw this as a way to transform the society eventually. And the movement was small, and it was embattled and endangered, and we had no idea it would ever be as successful as it was. But we knew this was a historic change, and I was always aware I was photographing history. And I took pictures other photographers didn't take, because I saw this as a historical movement that needed to be fully documented. And sometimes I used an assignment as a cover to do this. The one that comes most easily to mind was when Ross Barnett's term as the governor of Mississippi was up. He was succeeded by a very button-down, but equally segregationist guy named Paul Johnson. And *Time* assigned me to photograph Johnson's inauguration. So I arrived in the southern Mississippi political scene with my *Time* credentials. I was just another kid with a camera, but to me it was like landing on the surface of Mars. I mean, what I saw was so strange to my eyes. And I felt like I was a spy. I was taking pictures that seemed to me so damning that if anybody had the same consciousness, they would instantly kill me for doing what I was doing. But I was invisible because I was the *Time* magazine photographer. I was gonna get them publicity in a national magazine.

So the fall of '63 was pretty frightening. SNCC was holding their first mock election, because they could not register or participate in the regular elections but they wanted to show that black people would take part in the political process if they were allowed to. [Eventually] about eighty thousand Mississippi blacks voted in the mock election for governor. And they elected Aaron Henry as governor and Ed King as lt. governor—a black man and a white man. I started to work on the Aaron Henry campaign [for SNCC] in the fall of '63, and I went to Greenwood. I photographed some activities around the Greenwood office and then I went to a scary little Delta town called Belzoni. Before I went, I called up Hodding Carter, Jr., this was

before he worked for Lyndon Johnson. He was running his father's newspaper in Greenville, Mississippi. Greenwood was a really bad place, and Greenville was more tolerant. And Hodding Carter, a liberal Mississippian, had run the *Delta Democrat Times* most of his life. He took a lot of shit for that, but being [in] Greenville, he got away with it. So I called and I said, "Hodding, I'm going into Belzoni, what advice do you have for me?"—'cause I wanted to get out alive. He said, "Belzoni! You know what we say about Belzoni? If you want a carload of sons of bitches, you back a boxcar up to Belzoni and load on the first forty men you see!" Typical Mississippi invective. Funny and to the point. Danny [Lyon] and I went with Ronnie Dugger, who was a reporter and had a *Newsweek* assignment.

[In Belzoni] the first thing we saw was these three guys in a brand-new rental Pontiac who had driven in to bring a ballot box and convince people to take part in the mock election. COFO, the Council of Federated Organizations, which was largely SNCC in Mississippi, was trying to demonstrate that if allowed to take part in the political process, blacks would vote because the white wisdom was "our Negroes just aren't interested in voting." Two black people had over the previous decade tried to register to vote in Belzoni. They were both shot by the sheriff, one fatally. And that was the way Belzoni dealt with the voting issue. So these guys drove into a black neighborhood, set the ballot box up on the rear trunk of the Pontiac, and started preaching in the street, and a small, frightened group of black citizens gathered to watch them. Nobody moved. Shortly after [we arrived], the police drove up. We were shooting. I think that's the only time I shot with Danny. We'd shoot, then we'd get scared and climb back in the car, and then we'd get out and shoot some more. But the police arrived with the mayor, a very hard-bitten guy, and they ignored the SNCCers. They went straight to us; they wanted to see credentials. Ronnie had *Newsweek* credentials and we both had Birmingham police passes.

It's clear we influenced their actions because they were pretty circumspect. Otherwise they would have busted these guys immediately, beaten them up, and thrown them in jail. I don't think there's any question about that. But now they just parked directly behind their car. And their effect on the civil rights guys was dramatic. Willie Shaw, who was known as Preacher Shaw, sat on the hood of the Pontiac and started singing civil rights songs. Then under the eyes of the police, people began coming forward one by one, signing ballots and dropping them in the ballot box. It was electrifying to watch! What courage that took! We were all gonna be gone. They were gonna continue living in that town, but some people had finally had enough and said, "I'll sign your ballot." That went on for a while and then a policeman got out of his car and paced off the distance between the Pontiac and the nearest fire hydrant, and determined they were parking too close to the hydrant, and arrested them for that infraction. Took the ballot box, and I don't know whether they arrested everybody or just Willie. But we left town, and I think the SNCC car left town, too. And it was a very little scene, but I'll never forget it. Probably a lot of other people won't either, because that was how the movement worked, these little scenes in little towns. It just kind of filtered through the atmosphere in Mississippi, word of mouth, and people gradually got up the courage to move a little bit. [These were] local people who had been under this yoke for generations and [were] galvanized by fearless young black kids coming into the communities and doing stuff that just scared the shit out of me and everybody else who watched it. But it moved things on.

So events continued. In the spring of 1964 I began to hear plans to bring a thousand college students into the South, and I began to think, okay, what can I do? While living in Philadelphia I had made an attempt to start a [major, new] documentary project. I met with a couple of other photographers and we made plans and drew up a proposal, and we needed a Roy Striker[2] to run our project and we nominated Howard Chapnick who was then an editor of Black Star. Howard was quite intrigued. He was a major figure in magazine photojournalism at the time. But then the owners of

Black Star, two German Jews who had fled as the Nazis came into power and reestablished their European picture agency in New York, got ready to retire and they offered Howard the agency, and that was too good [for him] to pass up, and so our project died.

But I [still] had this goal in mind. And I was absolutely driven by this idea that I'd have a team of photographers in that state that summer. What I wanted was a two- or three-year project for which the summer would be a pilot and would demonstrate the feasibility of doing it. So I went to New York in June to fund-raise, and I was unsuccessful. I stopped to see Howard on the way out, and told him what I was doing; I should have done it first thing, but it didn't occur to me. Howard liked the idea, got on the telephone, and raised ten thousand dollars in fifteen minutes—ten thousand dollars was enough to do it in those days. I also saw Dorothea and asked her to become our Roy Stryker. She said, "It's too political [for me], but I'll act as an advisor." She was trying to start her own documentary project at the time, and although she didn't know it, she had contracted esophageal cancer, which would eventually kill her. But she was very encouraging. Then I put together a team initially of seven photographers. In the middle of the summer, I had to fire two of them, 'cause they weren't producing anything. But we were now ready to go.[3]

And once our project started, I [realized I] needed a base of operations, and so I moved [from Jackson] to Mileston, up in the Mississippi Delta. There was a good Freedom School there and Abe Osheroff[4] was building a community center, and I thought that was a good story. It also put me in the heart of the Mississippi Delta. And since Mileston was a community of independent black farmers, there was a bit of security there. And I felt like I needed that bit of security and a center of operations for what was going on.

And that summer suddenly SNCC was flush with money, because the friends of SNCC in the North were raising lots of funds and holding festivals. And everybody was pouring [in] money, and SNCC, which had been so impoverished, could rent a dozen cars or more. So Avis and Hertz were our friends, until we started sending cars back with bullet holes in them [laughs], then they weren't so enthusiastic about the whole thing. I don't want to overdramatize it. The day-to-day existence was more boring than anything else, but there were moments. And I was scared most of the time, and I was driven. I had a strong desire to advance my career as a photojournalist, to become good at what I was doing and to become known for what I was doing. And I was deeply committed to the cause. And all this just boiled within me. I was young, had lots of energy. Jeannine shared totally in all of this. She was probably a little more radical than I was, but I don't think we ever disagreed about basic stuff. And [as I said] I knew this was a historical moment, and I knew that I had an important role to play with my cameras.

And when I would go into a situation [to photograph], I would strap my cameras on like armor plate. They were my shield, my protection, and my reason for being there, and I could do things that would scare the shit out of me at other times, because I had a reason to be there. You know, I think all of us were acting beyond our capacity, called upon by the situation to surpass ourselves. I always felt like I could have done more in a situation. But I also felt, this is my job; I'll do the best I can and I'll pour everything I have into it. And when it was really working, I worked in an almost mindless state. There was a little corner in my brain that was saying FA at 250th, and all the lights are going down and I better take a meter reading, or I need lots of depth of field for the situation, or now let me grab the 24mm lens, there was that technical stuff going. As far as the aesthetics of the photographs, there was a little voice in my head saying, "No, no, no, yes." The voice was informed by this library of images that was there—because I had been looking at pictures intensely for the last eight years, or whatever it was. And I was always learning, and when I was on I was really on. I'd be exhausted at the end of a shooting situation, because I had poured everything I could into it. And I didn't realize until it was all over how intense it had been and how much of myself I had poured into it.

Those were my best pictures, you know. I rarely came that close to it ever again.

And the push was not: I'm a great photographer; I want to make great pictures. It was, this is a social movement that I believe in, and I'm going to help it the best way I can by taking the best pictures I can. This is what drove Danny [Lyon] or George [Ballis]. We were there because we were social activists, and we were social activists with cameras.

Initially, I tried to do things that were close at home, since I wanted to maintain this base and I needed it to maintain communication [with the other photographers] and give them assignments. I did extensive coverage of the Freedom School in Mileston. I did extensive coverage of the building of the community center. I photographed political meetings of the Mississippi Freedom Democratic Party. I traveled around to do that. But what was most amazing was watching the interaction [at the Freedom Schools] between the kids and the teachers, mostly white Ivy League students coming down, doing their first teaching ever and the kids having their first nonexploitative contact with white people. Watching what happened was quite amazing and how both groups of people flourished in that situation. The kids saw possibilities in their lives they'd never seen before. And they responded to these friendships and connections, and they just flowered. The local people also flowered but in more subdued ways. The kids were extraordinary, and I photographed kids in the Mileston Freedom School who went on to do quite interesting and significant things. There was one kid who became the mayor of Tchula, a little nearby town, and transformed the town. He was so bright and so obviously growing with every passing day that he was a very interesting subject to photograph. Mario Savio, who started the Free Speech Movement, was another summer volunteer in Mileston. I have pictures of Mario [Savio] taking a bath at the pump behind the Freedom House and shaving in the kitchen. He came out of Mississippi and went back to Berkeley and turned the campus upside down, and then turned campuses upside down all over the country. So that summer was electric. It was transformational in every way.

And I kept in touch with the movement even though I wasn't in Jackson, at the center. And the movement, as [James] Forman so presciently understood, depended upon the word getting out to the wider nation. These events had to reach a much wider audience. And we were the agents of that, at least for these pictures, which carried the strongest emotional message. And I understood that. Charlie Moore's photographs of the hosing and the police dogs attacking demonstrators in Birmingham were passed from hand to hand in the halls of [U.S.] Congress. And they had a direct result in the Civil Rights Act of 1964 being passed.[5] Those were critical pictures. I don't know that our pictures had [that impact], but they were published widely and they served to dramatize and publicize what was going on in the South to the nation at large. In the long run, it was only the cooperation of the nation at large that resulted in real change in the South. So everybody who was involved in this played a vital role in getting the word out. That's what we did.

And when I look back on it—you know, I photographed Greenpeace and I've a book on the AIDS quilt—but nothing I've done in my life was as significant as those photographs. And in the years hence I've spent a large portion of my life reprinting [these images] and creating a picture agency to get them out to the world. And I consider that the agency has two missions: one is to provide money to me and my photographers, who all need it, and most of whom are still involved in social causes. But the more important thing is that it educates the country about that moment in history, which is universally acknowledged as one of the pivotal turning points in U.S. history. There's nothing quite like the Civil Rights Movement where forces coalesced in a very limited period of time and people's lives were made better by what happened. Not perfect, but better. I'm sometimes a little bit nonplussed that so much of my subsequent life has been focused on those few years. But on the other hand, it's the most important thing I did. Probably. I mean, who

knows? We never know what we do. But it seems like that to me right now.

Notes

1. Women Strike for Peace was formed in 1961 to support a ban on nuclear testing. In 1962 women from the organization, including Coretta Scott King, traveled to Geneva, Switzerland, to be delegates to a seventeen-nation disarmament conference.

2. Roy Stryker, an economist by training, headed the Information Division of the Farm Security Administration during the Great Depression and launched the FSA's photodocumentary project. The project aimed to use images of the rural poor and the migrants from the dust bowl to support President Roosevelt's New Deal initiatives. The FSA project turned out to be effective on two levels. First, it was a definite spur to new legislation. Second, and perhaps more important, it produced a remarkable documentary portrait of ordinary American people caught in the crises of the Great Depression.

3. The remaining group of project photographers were: George Ballis, Dave Prince, Nick Lawrence, Danny Lyon, and Matt Herron.

4. Abraham Osheroff (1915–2008) was an American social activist, carpenter, and filmmaker, who helped build a community center in Holmes County, Mississippi.

5. Charlie Moore, initially a photographer working for two Montgomery papers, covered the Birmingham movement. U.S. Senator Jacob Javits said that Moore's photos "helped spur passage of the 1964 Civil Rights Act."

Bob Fletcher

Bob Fletcher became interested in photography while an undergraduate at Fisk University. He had always been drawn to the arts, but when his parents gave him a subscription to Norman Cousins's Saturday Review of Literature, *which featured the work of contemporary photographers like Gordon Parks and W. Eugene Smith and the images of the Farm Security Administration, he decided to try it himself.*

In 1963, while in graduate school, Fletcher spent the summer in Harlem as an organizer for the Harlem Education Project (HEP), an affiliate of the Northern Student Movement, and began photographing HEP activities and Harlem life. At the end of the summer, he took a year off from school to continue working with HEP. During the year, he was arrested while photographing a picket line and spent a night in the "Tombs," New York's infamous holding facility. In jail, he decided to become an education volunteer for the 1964 Mississippi Summer Project. "I thought, if I'm going to spend a night in jail for this bullshit, I'm going to go someplace where being in jail means something."

In Mississippi, Fletcher met the photographers of the Southern Documentary Project (SDP) and Cliff Vaughs, who was covering the Summer Project for SNCC. He gave up the idea of teaching and started traveling with Vaughs and documenting the activities of independent black farmers living in the Harmony community in Leake County, Mississippi. "I learned how to photograph in that process," Fletcher noted, "so my early photography was not that good because I didn't understand when to switch lenses or what lenses to use." At the end of the summer, Fletcher accompanied the MFDP delegation to Atlantic City. In the following year, he became a SNCC photographer, and he covered the demonstrations in Selma, Alabama, leading up to "Bloody Sunday" and its aftermath, the Selma to Montgomery march.

In 1966, Fletcher photographed the Meredith March and, later, covered the Lowndes County Freedom Organization's Freedom Vote. Also, from late 1965 to the fall of 1968, he worked with the Southern Visual Education Service, a SNCC media project established to develop filmstrips and related materials to be used as organizing tools.

In this role, he worked with Maria Varela to produce If You Farm, You Can Vote, a filmstrip designed to organize black cotton farmers and teach them how to vote in the federally funded cotton allotment elections (a benefit reserved until then for white farmers), and Something of Our Own, *a publication that encouraged local okra farmers to join the West Batesville, Mississippi, Farmers Co-op.*

In 1968 Fletcher relocated to New York City. Over the next two decades, he made his living as a professional photographer and documentary filmmaker. In 1987, he enrolled at the New York University law school and began a second career. Upon completion of his studies, he took the bar exam and began practicing law in New York. Currently, he's also licensed to practice in Texas, Florida, and New Jersey, and he commutes between the offices of his firm in New York and Florida.

David Prince

David Prince was born in Charleston, South Carolina, in 1942 and grew up in Yellow Springs, Ohio, where his father worked as a microbotanist for the developing national space program. Prince "turned to photography" in high school as a way to communicate and stay engaged in his classes. Upon graduating in 1960, he enrolled in Ohio University, the only four-year program in the U.S. granting degrees in photojournalism. He studied with the same teachers who taught documentary photographers Paul Fusco and James Karales and "aspired to become a Look or Life photographer."

As a university senior, Prince began traveling into the South to fulfill class assignments. "I was a weekend revolutionary," he says, "and even though I was living in the midst of some of the worst poverty in America, I had to discover poverty by going to Mississippi and Alabama." Prince's student photos eventually were published in the school newspaper and later found their way into a SNCC office, where Matt Herron discovered them and invited Prince to join the Southern Documentary Project (SDP).

Prince was the only full-time student in the project, which brought four other photographers into Mississippi to cover COFO's Freedom Summer. Early in July 1964, on the project's first days, Prince was assigned to accompany freelance writer Jerry DeMuth to a voter registration drive in Selma. The assignment turned the two young men into "movement legends" when they were beaten by Sheriff Jim Clark's posse and later involved in a United States Justice Department investigation of the incident.

After the Selma ordeal, Prince traveled to Philadelphia, Mississippi, and documented the family of murdered civil rights worker James Chaney; the new Freedom School in the community of Mound Bayou, Mississippi; and the plantation of Mississippi senator James Eastland, with its physically intact slave quarters. After the summer, Prince returned to Athens and graduated from Ohio University, gave up photography, and became a documentary film-maker. "I made some films for PBS," he said, "and then got enticed back to Ohio University, where I was hired as one of their professors and taught film for thirty years."

Reflecting on his tumultuous summer in Alabama and Mississippi, Prince wanted to clarify the nature of his SDP

involvement: "I didn't really think of myself as a profes-
sional photographer that summer, but as a freedom guy,
as someone who got on the front lines and got his hands
dirty. I thought of myself as a part of SNCC. We were actu-
ally paid through the SNCC offices, and I felt that I was a
movement person. That's how I want to be remembered."

Bob Adelman

A child of Jewish immigrants, Bob Adelman was born on October 30, 1930, in Brooklyn, New York, and raised in nearby Rockaway. His father, an amateur photographer, taught him how to use a darkroom and first piqued his interest in photography. "My father was a disciplined craftsman," Adelman said. "I learned precision from him. But all photographers originally get hooked on the magic—the shazam—of the way a blank piece of paper all of a sudden takes on an image."

Adelman earned an undergraduate degree from Rutgers University, where he majored in philosophy with a focus on aesthetics. For a brief time, he entertained the notion of becoming a lawyer, but was disillusioned "that the law had so little to do with justice." In the late 1950s, he became an assistant to commercial photographers, and then apprenticed with Alexey Brodovitch, the legendary Russian art director and graphic designer who taught photographers Richard Avedon and Diane Arbus. "Brodovich was a great influence," Adelman noted. "His aesthetics were simple—astonish me! Show me something I haven't seen before."

In the early 1960s, Adelman began taking social documentary photographs. "Like everyone else in the country," he said, "I had the idea that segregation was wrong. The courts had ruled it was illegal in schools, but it didn't do much good. The country was paralyzed. But when the students in the South began their sit-ins, I though that was an effective way to make change." Through friends, Adelman got in touch with the Congress of Racial Equality (CORE) and photographed their efforts to desegregate restaurants and bus terminals on Route 40, between New York and Washington DC.

Developing a long-term connection with CORE, Adelman wound up photographing such critical movement events as the 1963 March on Washington and SCLC's Project C in Birmingham, where he took his dramatic images of protestors being fire-hosed. "Lillian Smith once said to me," Adelman explained, "don't watch the whites. Whatever they are doing they've been doing for the last hundred years. Watch what the blacks are doing. They're taking their bodies to where they were not supposed to be. My Birmingham pictures were unique because that was my

*focus. And the fire hoses were brutal. They ripped the bark
from trees. But rather than being pushed around by them,
the people held onto one another and were able to resist
them. And, eventually, they stopped hosing them."*

*In the ensuing years, the major magazines discovered
Adelman's movement images, and he wound up photographing cover stories for* Esquire, Time, People, Life,
Harper's Magazine, The New York Times Magazine,
and Paris Match. *He has photographed or written more
than a dozen books, including* Mine Eyes Have Seen:
Bearing Witness to the Struggle for Civil Rights.
*His photographs have been exhibited at the Smithson-
ian, the American Federation of Art, and several other
institutions. They also are included in the collection of the
Museum of Modern Art.*

Recommended Reading

Blackwell, Unita, with JoAnne Prichard Morris. *Barefootin': Life Lessons from the Road to Freedom*. New York: Crown Publishers, 2006.

Carmichael, Stokely, with Ekwueme Michael Thelwell. *Ready for Revolution: The Life and Struggles of Stokely Carmichael (Kwame Ture)*. New York: Scribner, 2003.

Carson, Clayborne. *In Struggle: SNCC and the Black Awakening of the 1960s*. Cambridge Mass: Harvard University Press, 1982.

Cobb, Charles E., Jr. *On the Road to Freedom: A Guided Tour of the Civil Rights Trail*. Chapel Hill: Algonquin Books, 2008.

Crosby, Emilye. *A Little Taste of Freedom: The Black Freedom Struggle in Claiborne County, Mississippi*. Chapel Hill: University of North Carolina Press, 2005.

Curry, Constance, et al. *Deep in Our Hearts: Nine White Women in the Freedom Movement*. Athens: University of Georgia, 2000.

Dittmer, John. *Local People: The Struggle for Civil Rights in Mississippi*. Urbana: University of Illinois Press, 1994.

Emery, Kathy, Linda Reid Gold, and Sylvia Braselmann, eds. *Lessons from Freedom Summer: Ordinary People Building Extraordinary Movements*. Monroe, Maine: Common Courage Press, 2008.

Forman, James. *The Making of Black Revolutionaries*. Seattle: University of Washington Press, 1985.

Holsaert, S. Faith, et al. *Hands on the Freedom Plow: Personal Accounts by Women in SNCC*. Urbana: University of Illinois Press, 2010.

Hogan, Wesley C. *Many Minds, One Heart: SNCC's Dreams for a New America*. Chapel Hill: University of North Carolina Press, 2009.

Jeffries, Hasan Kwame. *Bloody Lowndes: Civil Rights and Black Power in Alabama's Black Belt*. New York: New York University Press, 2009.

King, Mary. *Freedom Song: A Personal Story of the 1960s Civil Rights Movement*. New York: William Morrow & Co., 1987.

Martínez, Elizabeth Sutherland. *Letters from Mississippi*. Brookline, MA: Zephyr Press, 2002.

McAdam, Doug. *Freedom Summer*. Oxford University Press, 1988.

Moody, Anne. *Coming of Age in Mississippi*. New York: Dell, 1968.

Moses, Robert P., and Charles E. Cobb, Jr. *Radical Equations: Civil Rights from Mississippi to the Algebra Project*. Boston: Beacon Press, 2001.

Moye, J. Todd. *Let the People Decide: Black Freedom and White Resistance Movements in Sunflower County, Mississippi, 1945–1986*. Chapel Hill: University of North Carolina Press 2004.

Payne, Charles M. *I've Got the Light of Freedom: The Organizing Tradition and the Mississippi Freedom Struggle*. Berkeley: University of California Press, 1995.

Payne, Charles M., and Carol Sills Strickland, eds. *Teach Freedom: Education for Liberation in the African-American Tradition*. New York: Teachers College Press, 2008.

Raiford, Leigh. *Imprisoned in a Luminous Glare: Photography and the African American Freedom Struggle* Chapel Hill: University of North Carolina Press. 2010.

Ransby, Barbara. *Ella Baker and the Black Freedom Movement: A Radical Democratic Vision*. Chapel Hill: University of North Carolina Press, 2003.

Schmeisser, Iris. "Camera at the Grassroots: The Student Nonviolent Coordinating Committee and the Politics of Visual Representation." In *The Civil Rights Movement Revisited: Critical Perspectives on the Struggle for Racial Equality in the United States*, ed. by Patrick B. Miller, Therese Frey Steffen, and Elizabeth Schäfer-Wünsche, Hamburg: Lit Verlag, 2001.

Sellers, Cleveland, with Robert Terrell. *The River of No Return: The Autobiography of a Black Militant and the Life and Death of SNCC*. Jackson: University of Press of Mississippi, 1990.

Watson, Bruce. *Freedom Summer: The Savage Season That Made Mississippi Burn and Made America a Democracy*. New York: Viking Adult Press, 2010.

Zellner, Bob, with Constance Curry. *The Wrong Side of Murder Creek: A White Southerner in the Freedom Movement*. Montgomery, Alabama: New South Press, 2008.

Index

Abernathy, Mrs. [Juanita], 165

Abernathy, Rev. Ralph David, 28, 107, 152–53, 154, 165–66

Activist photographers, 9–10

Adelman, Bob, 9, 12, 22–23, 56, 58–59, 84, 134–38, 243–44

AFL-CIO, 225

African American freedom struggle, 192, 195, 202

Alabama National Guard, 109

Albany, Georgia, 193

Atlanta, Georgia, 98–99, 153–60

Atlantic City, New Jersey, 88–96, 197

Baez, Joan, 100, 193

Baker, Ella, 13, 93, 97, 189, 202

Baker, Josephine, 193

Baldwin, James, 229

Ballis, George, 9, 12, 20, 68–69, 88–96, 128–29, 223–27, 237

Barnett, Ross, 235

Barry, Marion, 213–14

Batesville, Mississippi, 120–21

Battle of Midway, 225

Belafonte, Harry, 193

Belzoni, Mississippi, 235–36

Bernard, Lee, 104–5

Birmingham, Alabama, 97, 134–35, 136–37, 243–44

Birmingham 16th Street Baptist Church (bombing), 207–9

Black, Edie, 74

Black Belt, 28

Black Panther Party, 118, 122–25, 199–201

Black Power, 11, 15, 162, 168, 171, 180–81, 184–85, 188, 199–200

Black Star, 236

Block, Sam, 64, 195

Boebel, Jim, 78

Bogalusa, Louisiana, 142–45

Bond, Julian, 9, 12, 208, 210, 214

Brodovitch, Alexey, 243

Bunche, Dr. Ralph, 106–7

Bus Boycott, 97

Cambridge, Maryland, 193

Camden, Alabama, 58, 119

Canton, Mississippi, 121, 169, 182–85

Carmichael, Stokely, 118, 162, 165, 167–68, 177, 180–81, 193, 197, 199, 201

Carson, Clayborne, 11–12

Carter, Hodding, Jr., 235

Carthan, Eddie, 76

Chaney, Ben, 128

Chaney, Fannie Lou, 128, 130–31

Chaney, James Earl, 94, 128–29, 131, 227, 241

Chapnick, Howard, 236

Chavez, Cesar, 228

Chicago, Illinois, 99

Child Development Group of Mississippi (CDGM), 31, 43

Citizens Councils, 127

Citizenship Schools, 119

Civil Rights Acts: 1964, 162, 220, 238; 1965, 118, 121, 162, 198

Clark, Jim, 138, 219, 240

Clark, Septima, 119

Clarksdale, Mississippi, 87

Clinton, Louisiana, 58–59, 84

Cobb, Charlie, 11–12, 195

COINTELPRO, 201

Coleman, Woody, 196, 198

Coles, Robert, 219

Congress of Racial Equality (CORE), 10, 22, 128, 162, 165, 188, 196, 243

Council of Federated Organizations (COFO), 64–65, 68, 78, 82, 87, 132–33, 215
Crosby, Emilye, 12
Curry, Connie, 218

Dahmer, Vernon, 162, 215
Danville, Virginia, 193
Davis, Rennie, 220
Deacons for Defense, 142, 162
Democratic National Convention (1964), 87–96, 197
DeMuth, Jerry, 240
Dennis, Dave, 128–29
Devine, Annie, 164–65
Dittmer, John, 12
Du Bois, W. E. B., 15
Dugger, Ronnie, 235
Dylan, Bob, 193

Eastland, James, 194, 241
Eutaw, Alabama, 100
Evans, Walker, 21
Evers, Medgar, 60, 234

Farm Labor, 223
Farm Security Administration, 238–39
Farm Workers Movement (California), 225–26, 228
Farras, Christine, 157
Father Oulette, 219–20
Featherstone, Ralph, 122
Feinstein, Harold, 212
Finer, Dr. June, 146
Fitch, Bob, 9, 12, 19–20, 23–24, 29, 32–33, 34–35, 36–37, 38–39, 98–105, 119–20, 151–60, 163–68, 170–71, 173, 181, 183, 228–32
Fletcher, Bob, 9, 15, 22, 31–32, 37, 42–43, 46, 48–49, 54, 56–57, 122, 124–25, 221, 239–40
Fondren, El, 120–21
Forman, James, 15, 20, 208
Free Speech Movement, 76, 188, 229
Freedom Day, 56
Freedom Riders, 192, 194

Freedom Summer (Mississippi Summer Project), 14, 65, 71, 93, 195, 197, 212, 241
Fusco, Paul, 241

Gandhi, Mohandas, 98–99
Garrison, Jim, 233
Glide Foundation, 228
Goldwater, Barry, 194
Goodman, Andrew, 94, 131
Grassroots organizing, 28
Gray, Danny, 196
Gray, Victoria, 90
Green, Robert, 168
Greensboro Four, 192
Greenville, Mississippi, 235; air force base, 139–41
Greenwood, Mississippi, 56, 58–59, 60–61, 64, 181, 183, 193, 227, 235
Grenada, Mississippi, 36, 100–101
Guyot, Lawrence, 168

Haber, Al, 217
Hall, Robert, 196
Hamer, Fannie Lou, 60, 65, 88, 197, 227
Hardy, John, 195
Harlem Education Project (HEP), 239
Harmony, Mississippi, 42
Hattiesburg, Mississippi, 66–67, 79–83, 90, 212–16
Hawthorne, Gracie, 78–79
Hayden, Casey, 218–19, 221
Hayden, Tom, 217
Hayes, Curtis, 195
Henry, Aaron, 87, 195, 235
Herbert, Lee, 127
Herron, Jeannine, 234
Herron, Matt, 9, 11, 41, 43, 46–47, 50–55, 61, 64, 74–78, 80, 107–17, 121, 142–50, 169, 171, 177–81, 183–84, 186–87, 221, 233–38, 241
Heschel, Rabbi Abraham Joshua, 107
Heston, Charlton, 193
Holland, Ida Mae, 61
Holloway, Joe, 230

Holmes County, Michigan, 126

Holmes County Freedom Democratic Party, 126

Hulett, John, 199

Humphrey, Hubert, 89

Indianola, Mississippi, 63

Jackson, Jane, 121

Jackson, Jimmie Lee, 106, 198

Jackson, June, 121

Jackson, Mahalia, 193

Jackson, Mississippi, 55, 68–69, 146–50, 180–81, 183–84

Japanese Canadian Centennial Project, 206

Javits, Jacob, 194, 238

Jim Crow system, 191

Johnson, June, 182–83

Johnson, Lyndon Baines, 89–91, 109, 118, 197–98

Johnson, Paul, 146, 235

Karales, James, 241

Karenga, Ron (Maulana), 199

Kelly Ingram Park (Birmingham, Alabama), 101–2, 104, 134–35

Kennedy, John F., 134, 233

King, Alberta Williams, 156–57

King, Alfred Daniel, 152–53

King, Bernice, 158–59

King, Coretta Scott, 151–55, 157–59, 165

King, Ed, 234–35

King, Martin Luther, III, 102, 152–53, 158

King, Rev. Martin Luther, Jr., 28, 89, 97–108, 151–61, 162, 164–68, 177, 192; "I Have a Dream" speech, 195, 199, 202–4; "Mountain Top" speech, 228, 230

King, Rev. Martin Luther, Sr., 156

King, Mary, 68–69

King, Yolanda, 102, 158

Krohn, Huey, 146–47

Ku Klux Klan, 60, 63, 94, 127, 131–32, 162

Landerman, Dick, 82

Lange, Dorothea, 21, 226–27, 229, 236

Lawson, James, 194

Leatherer, Jim, 112–13

Lee, Bernard, 104–5, 167–68

Lee, Herbert, 127

Leigh, Sandy, 67, 212

Lelyveld, Rabbi Arthur, 20, 83, 212, 215

Lester, Julius, 16

Lewis, John, 108–9, 193–94, 197, 199, 201, 208, 211

Listening Eye Gallery, 233

Little Rock Nine, 192

Liuzzo, Viola, 231–32

Loveman's Department Store, 136–37

Lowndes County, Alabama, 116–17, 118, 122–25

Lowndes County Freedom Organization (LCFO), 14, 118, 122–25, 199, 239

Lyon, Danny, 208–10, 235, 237

Malcolm X, 198

Mants, Bob, 199

March on Washington, 192–95

McComb, Mississippi, 195

McKissik, Floyd, 162, 165, 177

McLaurin, Charles, 195

McNeal Elementary School (Canton, Mississippi), 177, 179

Medical Committee for Human Rights, 146

Meredith, James, 162–63

Meredith March against Fear, 239

Meridian, Mississippi, 128–29

Mileston, Mississippi, 74–75, 76–78

Mileston Freedom House, 76

Mileston Freedom School, 74–76, 237–38

Mississippi, 226

Mississippi Freedom Democratic Party (MFDP), 88–96, 97, 188, 197, 237, 239

Mississippi Freedom Labor Union, 37, 63

Mondale, Walter, 89

Montgomery, Alabama, 97, 106

Montgomery Bus Boycott, 192

Moore, Amzie, 195

Moore, Charlie, 23, 238

Morehouse College, 209

Moses, Bob, 88, 132–33, 195, 198, 201–2, 214, 227

Moton, Leroy, 231–32

Mound Bayou, Mississippi, 63

Mt. Zion United Methodist Church, 131

NAACP, 60, 67, 87, 162, 188, 192

Nance, Jim, 81

National Student Association, 192–93

Neshoba County, Mississippi, 130–33

Newton, Huey P., 118

Nonviolent Action Committee (N-VAC), 196–99

Northern Student Movement, 239

Operation Bootstrap, 200

Osheroff, Abe, 236, 238

Pacific School of Religion, 228–29

Parks, Rosa, 151–52

Peacock, Willie, 195

Peter, Paul, and Mary, 193

Pettway, Maggie Lee, 58

Philadelphia, Mississippi, 197, 241

Poitier, Sidney, 193

Potter, Paul, 218–20

Prettyman, Julie, 213

Price, Cecil, 132

Prince, David, 12, 130–32, 241–42

Pugh, Hattie Mae, 82

Quinn, Anthony, 146–47

Quinn, Aylene, 146–47

Quitman County, Mississippi, 28

Randall, Herbert, 9, 12, 20, 66–67, 70–71, 78–79, 81–83, 212–16

Randolph, A. Philip, 193

Reeb, Rev. James, 198

Reuther, Walter, 166

Richardson, Judy, 12, 199

Ricks, Willie, 167

Rosedale, Mississippi, 43–44

Samuelson, Charles, 196

Savio, Mario, 76–77, 237–38

Schulke, Flip, 230

Schwerner, Michael "Mickey," 94, 131

Seale, Bobby, 118

Selma, Alabama, 106–7, 136, 138, 219–20

Selma to Montgomery March, 106–17, 197–98, 229

Shaw, Willie, 236

Shuttlesworth, Rev. Fred, 104–5

Simmons, Bobby, 110–11

Sims, Jamie, 41

Sit-in protests (1960), 192, 194

Sixteenth Street Baptist Church (Birmingham, Alabama), 102, 234

Smith, Doug, 215

Smith, Frank, 219

Smith, Lillian, 243

Smith, Scott B., 199

Southern Christian Leadership Conference (SCLC), 10, 19, 97; "People-to-People" tour, 102, 152–53, 188, 228, 230–32

Southern Documentary Project (SDP), 221–22, 223, 233, 239, 241

Southern Freedom Movement, 9, 28, 194

Southwest Georgia, 85–86

Spelman College, 209

St. Paul's Missionary Baptist Church, 50–52

Stryker, Roy, 236, 238

Student Nonviolent Coordinating Committee (SNCC), 10, 13–17, 60, 65, 97, 118, 122, 132–33, 165, 183, 188, 192–203, 208–11, 217–22, 223, 226–27, 235–38, 240–41; use of photographs, 10, 15–16, 20

Student Voice, The, 15, 196, 209

Students for a Democratic Society, 188, 192, 217–19

Tchula, Mississippi, 76

Tear gas attack, 178–79

Travis, Jimmy, 60, 64

U.S. Bureau of Reclamation, 223

U.S. Justice Department, 139

US Organization, 200

Valley View, Mississippi, 46–47, 50–53

Varela, Maria, 9, 12, 20–21, 24–25, 40–41, 44–45, 123–24, 126, 139–41, 171–72, 174–77, 182–85, 217–22, 240

Vaughs, Cliff, 239

Vaugn, Willie, 199

Wakayama, Tamio, 9, 19, 21, 26–27, 30–31, 34, 39, 62–63, 72–73, 85–86, 133, 206–11, 212

Walker, Walt and Jane, 197

Wallace, George, 109

Washington County, Mississippi, 138–41

Watkins, Hollis, 195

Watts "riot," 198–99

Werner, Peter, 66–67

Western College for Women (Oxford, Ohio), 65, 69–73

Williams, Hosea, 100, 104–5, 167, 230

Wilson, Doris, 113–15

Women Strike for Peace, 234, 238

Young, Andrew, 100, 105, 168, 230

Young Christian Students (YCS), 217–18

YWCA, 218